WORLD WAR TWO

MILITARY VEHICLES

TRANSPORT & HALFTRACKS

WORLD WAR TWO
MILITARY VEHICLES

G. N. GEORGANO

OSPREY
AUTOMOTIVE

Published in Great Britain in 1994 by Osprey,
an imprint of Reed Consumer Books Limited,
Michelin House, 81 Fulham Road, London SW3 6RB
and Auckland, Melbourne, Singapore and Toronto.

Reprinted Summer 1998.

ISBN 1 85532 406 7

Originated & produced by The Book Package Company Ltd.
Bournemouth, England.
Editor: David McKinney
Design: Justin Smith
Jacket colour separations by Appletone Graphics Ltd.
Bournemouth, England.

Typesetting and page make-up by The Madhouse Ltd.
Ringwood, England.

Set in 10pt on 11.5pt Monotype Bembo.

Produced by Toppan Printing Co., (H.K.) Ltd.
Printed and bound in China.

A C K N O W L E D G M E N T S

I owe a great debt to the work of the doyen of military vehicle historians, Bart Vanderveen. His *Military Vehicles Directory* and the many excellently-researched articles in his quarterly magazine, *Wheels & Tracks*, have provided invaluable sources of information. I would also like to thank Fred Crismon, leading historian of the American military vehicle, Nick Baldwin, Tony Fletcher, Bill Ladbrooke, Elizabeth Nagle-Turnbull, Raymond Vaes and Jonathon Wood.

Also thanks to George Alexander and Roy Halsall of the Military Vehicle Conservation Group (Dorset) for loaning their vehicles and helping to locate others for photography.

For photographs I owe a debt to the staffs of the Imperial War Museum (IWM), National Motor Museum (NMM) and the Tank Museum, Bovington, Dorset.

The publishers and author particularly want to thank the Victory Memorial Museum, Aire Victory, Motorway E25/411, Belgium, for generously providing so many colour photographs of the vehicles at their museum.

G.N. Georgano

Repair compound on the 'Red Ball Express' route, 1944.

CONTENTS

CHAPTER ONE

Great Britain

By the end of the war the total number of
soft-skinned military vehicles used by the British armed sevices
was about one and a quarter million.

The British have never been happy with large standing armies or heavy military spending in peacetime, and consequently relatively little money or resources were devoted to up-to-date military vehicles in the interwar years. Numerous prototypes were built and the Army was always ready to test them, but substantial orders were seldom forthcoming. The public attitude changed somewhat in 1936 in the wake of Mussolini's conquest of Ethiopia and Hitler's occupation of the Rhineland, but the Abdication of King Edward VIII in December 1936, followed by the Coronation of his brother, concentrated attention on domestic matters again. In the words of Winston Churchill, "Foreign affairs and the state of our defences lost all claim upon the public mood. Our Island might have been ten thousand miles away from Europe."

In the Spring of 1939 the Government set up the Ministry of Supply to co-ordinate the production of military equipment of all kinds. This step had been recommended by Churchill three years earlier, and replaced a cumbersome system whereby vehicles for the RASC (Royal Army Service Corps) were ordered by the Quarter Master General, and other wheeled vehicles by the Master General of the Ordnance. Before the formation of the Ministry of Supply up to ten separate contracts were required for a single vehicle - for the chassis, body, cab and canvas tilt, even down to the towing hooks. Nevertheless, some specifically military designs were developed in the 1930s, mainly in the 15cwt 4x2 class (Morris Commercial CS8, Guy Ant and Bedford W) and 3-ton 4x2 or 6x4 (AEC Marshal, Crossley, Leyland Terrier, Thornycroft).

The numbers of trucks available to the Army were greatly increased by two schemes. There were two private companies which held a number of military-type vehicles normally used for forestry work which were hired out to the Army for their autumn manoeuvres. The other scheme was the simple one of compiling a register of suitable civilian vehicles which could be impressed into Army service when needed. About 26,000 vehicles were impressed in 1939, of which approximately 5,000 were private cars, 7,000 motorcycles and 14,000 trucks.

The total number of vehicles held by the War Department in 1939, including the above, was 55,000. A large number of these were sent to France with the British Expeditionary Force and most had to be left behind during the evacuation of troops at Dunkirk. This created an enormous need for vehicles which was made up partly by increased home production and also by the supply of vehicles from the United States and the Commonwealth. By the end of the war the total number of soft-skinned military vehicles used by the British armed services was about one and a quarter million.

Staff Cars

A considerable variety of cars was used by the Army, Navy and Air Force, swelled by many

impressed civilian cars. At the outbreak of war there
were 4,285 of the latter compared with 3,803 cars
specifically ordered by the forces, but by June 1940
the figures were 2,315 and 12,660 respectively.
About 8,000 cars of all kinds were left behind in
France, so it can be seen that a large number were
manufactured during the first nine months of the war.

The most popular small cars were the Austin
Ten, Hillman Minx, Standard Ten and Vauxhall
Fourteen, all of which were very similar to civilian
cars. Modifications were restricted to painting in
service livery, which included covering over all
chrome parts such as hubcaps, radiator shells and
headlamps. The Vauxhalls had their bonnet flutes
painted over. These smaller saloon cars were used
mostly on the Home Front, for transporting staff
officers and War Department officials, as they were
not suitable for the road conditions of overseas.
Vauxhalls, including Ten, Twelve and Twenty-Five
models, were used by the Army, Navy and RAF,
while Hillman Minxes were sent mainly to the
Navy and RAF and Standards only to the RAF.

The best known larger staff cars were made by
Ford and Humber. The Fords varied from civilian-
type American models of 1938 to 1942, to the
WOA1 saloon and WOA2 heavy utility. The civilian types were Fordor sedans powered by the 3.6-
litre 85bhp V8 engine, and differed from the
standard offering in having oversize 9.00x13 tyres.
Some of these were assembled by Ford's British factory at Dagenham and they saw service with the
Army and RAF in many theatres of war. Some

found their way to Russia and the author encountered one in Moscow in 1962, still on its chunky
tyres. The WOA1 and WOA1/A were specifically
army models which used the Four Light saloon
body of the pre-war British V8-22 with the big V8
engine and a military pattern radiator. The latter
they shared with the WOA2, a rugged looking
estate car classed by the Army as a heavy utility.
These had four side doors and a full-width rear
door which was split horizontally. There were two
rows of seats, with two tip-up seats in the rear cor-
ners, so a maximum of seven passengers could be
carried. Behind the bucket-type front seats a folding map table was provided, essential for the staff car
use to which the WOA2 was usually put. A few
were modified as open tourers for desert work. A
total of 11,754 WOA2 heavy utilities were made
from May 1941 to 1947.

Humbers were widely used as staff cars in a variety
of forms, though all were powered by the familiar
4086cc six-cylinder side-valve engine, introduced in
1926 on the Snipe. In 1939 the Rootes brothers
combined this engine with the 9ft 6in wheelbase
chassis of the Sixteen to make the Super Snipe, and
this was the basis for the Snipe staff car which went
into production in December 1939. The Super
Snipe was specifically intended to compete with
the American cars which were selling so well in
England, so it was an obvious choice for the Army
as an alternative to the Ford V8. The military Snipe
differed from the civilian model in a number of
ways. The most obvious was that the back of the

Right: **The militarised version of the Humber Super Snipe was known as the Snipe Mark II. It was made as a saloon, tourer, utility and light truck. This tourer has a very distinguished load, Winston Churchill (standing), seated next to him Field Marshal Alexander and in front Field Marshal Montgomery.** *(NMM)*

Above: **A Ford WOA2/A heavy utility in military camouflage in the service of the Post Office Telephones, Home Counties Division. The Post Office acquired a number of reconditioned ex-army vehicles in 1946, but the headlamp masks indicate wartime use, so it was probably bought new.** *(Telecom Showcase)*

body was cut away so that the mudguards would clear the ground even when the car was climbing a steep gradient such as a ramp. The springs were set up to give a greater ground clearance, which was 8$\frac{1}{2}$in with a full load, and the track was increased to 5ft $\frac{1}{2}$in at the front and 5ft 1in at the back. As on the Fords, 9.00x13 Dunlop Trak tyres were generally worn, running at a pressure of only 20psi. Sound-deadening trim such as thick carpets was absent in the military version and when Laurence Pomeroy tested one for *The Motor* in 1943, he found much more evidence of machinery at work than in the Super Snipe he had driven in 1939. However, in general, he was very impressed with the staff car, finding the 15 to 1 bottom gear capable of pulling away even on the worst gradient and surface he could find. Synchromesh was found on

the top two speeds only, but the lower two ratios were seldom needed, "...a matter of no mean importance when choosing a car for Army duties, bearing in mind the difficulties of securing adequate numbers of well trained drivers". The well protected 14-gallon fuel tank gave a range of between 200 and 250 miles.

Most Snipe staff cars were saloons, but open tourers were also made for desert work. The most famous of these was 'Old Faithful', a 1941 model which served Field Marshal Montgomery in the 8th Army throughout his North African campaign from El Alamein onwards, and in Italy as far as the Sangro. This car still exists and is on show at the Museum of Army Transport, Beverley, Yorks. Just after the war, a small number of Snipes were fitted with saloon bodies by Karmann of Osnabruck, for use by the British occupying forces. These originated as 8cwt trucks known as FFWs (Fitted For Wireless); with the end of hostilities they were no longer needed for these duties, but there was a serious shortage of staff transport, so it seemed logical to take advantage of skilled coachbuilders on the spot. Karmann, which had been founded in 1874, later made the famous Karmann-Ghia Volkswagen coupés, and today produces convertible versions of the VW Golf. Although outside the scope of this book, it is worth mentioning that a small number of armoured bodied cars based on the Humber Snipe were made in 1940. These were luxuriously fitted out by the Thrupp & Maberly coachbuilding firm for use by the Royal Family and Cabinet Ministers and were known as Special Ironside Saloons.

Above: **Field Marshal Montgomery standing up in his Humber Tourer, while crossing a pontoon bridge over the Seine at Vernon, near Beauvais, 1 September 1944.** *(IWM)*

Left: **The militarised Super Snipe saloon, the Mark II, went into production in December 1939.** *(Bart Vanderveen Collection)*

A few lightly modified Humber Pullman limousines were used by 'top brass' of the services, but the most important Humber apart from the Snipe was the 4x4 heavy utility. This was a remarkable vehicle, being the only four-wheel-drive machine of its size made in Britain at the time. It was intended for the same type of work as the Ford WOT2, being able to transport staff officers at high speed (maximum 63mph) over good roads and at the same time to keep going where roads were non-existent, on sand or deep mud. Although purpose-built for military needs, the Humber used many components from civilian vehicles, including the 4-litre Snipe engine and transverse leaf independent front suspension. The Snipe's four-speed gearbox was also used, drive then passing via a Layrub jackshaft to a transfer box, from the base of which universally-jointed shafts ran to the front and rear axles. The transfer box enabled the car to run with two-wheel drive on metalled roads, and to switch to four-wheel drive on a lower set of ratios for cross-country work. The steel and wood body was of estate-car type, with four doors at the sides and a divided panel at the back; the upper part, with two small windows, could be swung open, and the lower part let down as a tailboard. Normal seating capacity was seven, but the main rear seats and the inward facing occasional seats could be folded to make a flat platform if necessary. A folding map table was also provided.

The Humber heavy utility was a large vehicle, turning the scales at 2 tons $7\frac{1}{2}$cwt, compared with

1 ton 13cwt for the Snipe saloon and 1 ton $11\frac{1}{2}$cwt for the Ford WOT2, but it had a very satisfactory road performance. Comfortable cruising speed was 50mph, and *The Autocar* road tester found that it needed no more gear changing over normal roads than a 14 or 16hp saloon. To change to four-wheel drive all that was necessary was to double declutch, increase engine speed and pull the transfer lever upwards. This gave a lower set of ratios, top gear being 7.24 with four-wheel drive engaged, compared with 4.89 with rear drive only. Maximum speed on the lower ratios was about 40mph, but its cross-country performance was remarkable, and seemed astonishing to *The Autocar* in 1943, when four-wheel-drive cars were virtually unknown apart from the much smaller Jeep. They found that bomb craters presented no problems so long as there was not very deep water at the bottom, while the smooth bottom of the chassis allowed the car to slide on its belly over projecting ground without suffering damage. A loose-surfaced gradient of 1 in 2.5 was climbed with ease.

Variants on the Humber 4x4 included a general staff officers' version with improved interior comfort, map-reading lamp and a sliding roof, and a 'cross-country saloon' with car-type boot. The latter was made by Thrupp & Maberly, who had been responsible for the more expensive bodies on pre-war Humber cars and also made an ambulance version of the Humber 4x4. Still other variants, made in relatively small numbers, were an 8cwt general service truck and an armoured car. The Humber

was widely used in the North African campaign and on the Western Front. They were also used by the RAF Mountain Rescue Service which was formed during 1942 in North Wales. About 6500 were made of all versions and production ended in 1945. *The Autocar* observed that "it was the kind of car to have a strong appeal after the war to farmers or to large estates". Alas the Rootes brothers did not make a civilian version, leaving it to Rover to take up the challenge, though the early Land Rovers were much more spartan and cramped vehicles than the Humber.

Apart from the cars described so far, all of which were used in reasonable numbers, a great variety of other makes and models also saw service, mainly impressed vehicles used in the early days of the war. The RAF alone had some 100 models of 25 different makes, including a Bentley in Belfast and a Rolls-Royce limousine at Hawarden, near Chester. Field Marshal Montgomery had a Rolls-Royce Phantom III with unusual sport limousine body by H J Mulliner, with a reverse sloping wind-screen. Used by Field Marshal Lord Gort as a staff car from September 1939, it later passed to 'Monty' whose personal property it became.

Lightweight 4x2 & 4x4 vehicles

The war in the Far East revealed a need for an ultra-light Jeep-type vehicle capable of being dropped by parachute and also of being manhandled by the crew out of difficult situations. In America, Crosley, Chevrolet, Willys and Kaiser all produced prototypes of 'mini Jeep', and in England SS and Standard entered the field. SS Cars (Jaguar Cars Ltd from 1945 onwards) built two prototypes under the direction of Claude Baily, later chief designer for Jaguar, and Walter Hassan, who became chief engineer with Coventry Climax.

Their first design was a curious little machine intended to be compared with the heavy motorcycle combination. SS had started as sidecar makers, and during the war sidecars for use with 496cc BSA M20 motorcycles were made in large numbers. Known as the VA, the SS 'mini-Jeep' was powered by a 1096cc V-twin JAP engine located on the rear offside of the light pressed-steel body/chassis unit, driving the gearbox by roller chain, with final drive to the rear axle also by chain. It was almost square in plan view, with a wheelbase of 4ft 7in and track of 4ft 5in. Overall length was only 7ft 6in, and the VA weighed less than 8cwt. It was strictly a two-seater, with accommodation for a gunner next to the driver who sat on the left. At first, steering was by handlebars but later a wheel was substituted. The concentration of weight at the rear gave it very good traction, and the front end was so light that it could easily be lifted by one man. The only place for cooling vents for the air-cooled engine was behind the gunner, and cooling problems were the main reason for the failure of the VA as a practical replacement for the military motorcycle combination.

Above: **Humber 4x4 heavy utility in its most common form, a four-door estate car with divided panel at the rear. Other versions included an 8cwt truck, ambulance (see page 46), and armoured reconnaissance vehicle.** *(IWM)*

Above: **More powerful than the British 'Tillies' was the Ford WOC1, an Anglo-American design using the chassis of the American Ford V8 light commercial with British-built open-cab bodies made by Briggs. Just 2000 were built between December 1939 and July 1940, when the WOC1 was dropped in favour of the 15cwt WOT2. This one is at a Battery Command Post during combined manœuvres of the Royal Artillery and King's Shropshire Light Infantry.** *(IWM)*

Built in 1943, the single VA prototype was replaced before the year was out by the more conventional VB. The VB was a little bit larger, with a length of 8ft and weight of 8½cwt, and was powered by a front-mounted four-cylinder Ford Ten engine, driving through a Ford gearbox with an auxiliary gearbox giving a total of six forward speeds. Like the VA, the VB had all-round coil independent suspension, that at the rear being not unlike the Jaguar E-Type's of eighteen years later. The four-seater VB performed well, but was not put into production because the increased carrying capacity of aircraft removed the need for a small supply vehicle. Although produced by the same design team, the VA and VB were very different in purpose, for the latter was essentially a general purpose carrier and not a fighting vehicle, as was the machine gun equipped VA.

A similar concept to the VA was the JAB (Jungle Airborne Buggy) made by Standard in 1944. This was a tiny vehicle, only 6ft 6in long, powered by a four-cylinder Standard Eight engine. Unlike the SS machines, which were private ventures, the JAB was evolved by the Standard Motor Co Ltd in conjunction with the Directorate of Mechanisation at the Ministry of Supply. It was about as basic a motor vehicle as one could imagine, with virtually no

bodywork and a canvas cover for the engine. Seating for the crew of four was on motorcycle saddles. The motorcycle theme was also seen in the twist-grip accelerator on a crossbar above the engine. This was used to avoid the varied pressure on a foot accelerator which occurs when the driver is jolted about over rough ground. Both 4x2 and 4x4 prototypes were built, and the latter could climb a loose surfaced gradient of 1 in 2.4 fully laden. The wheels were fitted with modified 7.50x10 Spitfire aircraft tyres. The JAB was virtually an amphibious vehicle, as it pulled a two-wheeled trailer into which the front wheels could be placed. With the rear wheels dangling behind, the crew then paddled it across any stretch of water they might encounter. How this would have worked in combat conditions, in a fast flowing Burmese river for instance, was never known. There was not time enough to develop it before the war ended. A civilian development with tubular chassis and a greater length of 7ft 10in was planned in 1945, to be sold as the farmer's general purpose vehicle. The planned price was £100 to £140 which was extremely modest, but the project never got off the ground.

Standard also made a larger, 12hp engined, 5cwt general purpose vehicle very similar in size to

the American Jeep, but as it lacked four-wheel drive it was not competitive, and anyway by 1943 the Jeep was widely available to British forces.

Light Utilities

In this category came the most popular light load carriers used by all three services. They were all based on passenger car designs, the most common being the Austin Ten, Hillman Ten, Morris Series M and Standard Twelve. Behind the two-seater cab was an open truck body of the type known in America as a pick up, with canvas tilt cover supported by three hoopsticks. Some had two or four additional folding seats in the body, making them into four- or six-seater personnel carriers. A number of the latter on the Austin Ten were supplied to the Home Guard in 1940.

The Austin Utility, or 'Tilly' as they were popularly called, differed from the civilian car in a number of ways. The cylinder diameter was increased from 63.5 to 66.5mm, giving a capacity of 1237cc compared with 1125cc of the car. This gave more power, but was unacceptable on a private car as it would have lifted it from the 10 to 11hp taxation bracket. Lower gear ratios were provided, and the

'Tilly' had also a water pump, unlike its civilian counterpart, which relied on thermosyphon cooling. The lower overall gear ratios meant that its comfortable cruising speed was no more than 35mph 'to any driver with an ear for an engine', according to *The Autocar*'s H S Linfield. Large section 16x6.00 tyres were fitted and the spare wheel was carried on the roof of the cab. For liaison work a two-seater version of the Austin Eight tourer was made, with a load carrying space in place of the civilian car's rear seats.

The Hillman light utility was based on the 1940 model Minx and was very similar to the Commer delivery van. All commercial Hillmans for the civilian market were badged as Commers, yet for some reason the military version was called a Hillman. It was widely used by the Army and Royal Air Force and was made in six different models, varying in detail, from 1940 to 1945.

The Morris light utility was based on the 10hp Series M saloon which, like the 1940 Hillman Minx, had unitary construction. The cab was formed in unit with the chassis, while the pickup body was built separately. Unlike the Austin, the Morris 'Tilly' had no modifications from the standard car specifications, apart from moving the water pump to the front of the cylinder head and

Above: **The Quad-Ant was a 4x4 version of the Ant. Made in GS truck form from 1944, the chassis was originally for an artillery tractor as seen here. It can be identified as a tractor by the winch rope guide rollers on the front bumper.** *(IWM)*

15

Above: **Morris Commercial C8/GS 4x4 with the 62nd Anti-Tank Regiment, exercising near Tilshead on Salisbury Plain.** *(IWM)*

Right: **An MWD negotiating what was called a second class road, but had deteriorated into a muddy swamp, in Italy, north west of Termoli, during the Eighth Army's advance in 1943.** *(NMM)*

Left: **The standard Bedford MWD 15cwt truck in its most familiar form. Earlier versions had twin aero screens which gave very poor visibility when the cape cart hood was erected. MWs were used by all three services, and were purchased in bulk by the Ministry of Supply, who then allocated them to the Army, Navy or Royal Air Force.**
(NMM)

the replacement of the SU carburettor by a Solex. Larger section tyres were fitted and all but the earliest models had a plain wire mesh grille. Morris Utilities were among the many vehicles left behind after the evacuation of Dunkirk and were 'conscripted' into the German Army. Some were still in use in 1944 and were recaptured by the British for a further spell of active service.

The Standard Twelve was the basis for several light military vehicles. Vans for the RAF had car-type cabs and radiator grilles, while the Army's utilities had canvas topped cabs which were part of the main canvas body top, and much plainer wire mesh grilles. Both versions were used as ambulances.

The 'Tillys' performed sterling service in conditions for which their chassis had never been designed, for although they were not intended for cross-country work their use as general dogsbodies frequently took them off metalled roads, and the latter were not much fun to negotiate when they were pitted with shell holes. Distortions and fractures of chassis were frequent, as were breakages of axles and suspension units. (The Standard's transverse-leaf independent front suspension was soon replaced by old fashioned semi-elliptics). The other drawback of these civilian-based vehicles was that their low power/weight ratio led to excessive use of the gearbox. After supplies of the Jeep came on stream, the 'Tilly' was largely replaced for front line work, although they had better carrying capacity and weather protection than any Jeep.

Other uses for car-based vans were as mobile canteens run by the YMCA and similar organisations; vehicles used for this purpose included the Standard Eight and Ford E83W.

Light Trucks up to 15cwt

One of the most important types of vehicle used by the British Army was the 15cwt GS (General Service) truck. In 1933 the War Office laid down specifications for a new type of purpose-built truck for carrying loads up to 15cwt using standard, commercially built components as far as possible, with a short wheelbase, good ground clearance and a semi-forward driver's compartment. Five British manufacturers tendered vehicles, Morris Commercial, Ford, Commer, Guy and Vauxhall (Bedford). Of these, Morris Commercial were the first to produce a truck, the CS8, which was powered by the 3495cc 60bhp six-cylinder engine used in many civilian models. It had a wheelbase of 8ft 2in and weighed 1ton 18¼cwt in its standard GS form. Following the War Office specification, weather protection was simply a tarpaulin cover

Above: **The gun-carrying version of the MW was known as the MWG, but this is an early example on an MWD chassis. It is fitted with a 20mm Polsten anti-aircraft gun. Note the twin aero screens of the early MW models.** *(NMM)*

over the load-carrying area, and a folding canopy over the open cab. Early models had a low radiator and sharply sloping bonnet, but this was later modified to give the familiar multi-angle shape.

The CS8 was introduced in 1934 and was phased out in about 1941 in favour of the C4 which used a four-cylinder 3.5-litre engine but was otherwise similar. There was also an 8cwt version known as the PU8 and its 4x4 equivalent, the PU 8/4. These had the same six-cylinder engine as the CS8 and, being rated for a smaller load capacity, had a better performance, but early on in the war the Army decided to eliminate the 8cwt category in order to reduce the number of different types in service. No PUs were made after 1941.

The main variations on the basic CS8 were a fire tender, mobile office, fuel or water tanker, wireless truck and portee for two-pounder anti-tank gun. In the early years of the war, cab comfort was improved, with a fixed windscreen and metal doors in place of canvas. There was also an armoured version known as the AC9, of which 100 were made, seeing service with the British Expeditionary Force and in the Middle East.

Some of the bodies fitted to the Morris Commercials were too long and heavy for the 8ft 2in wheelbase, causing severe handling problems.

Above: **A column of Bedford MWGs with anti-aircraft guns.**
(The Tank Museum, Bovington)

Left: **A Bedford MWG anti-tank Portee being loaded with a 2 pounder anti-tank gun. When not in use the loading ramps were carried in outrigger brackets on each side of the body.**
(The Tank Museum, Bovington)

Above: **Fordson WOT2E** undergoing water-proofing tests under the watchful eyes of soldiers who might soon be depending on its water reliability. A total of 59,498 of the WOT series was made between December 1939 and December 1945.
(Ford of Britain)

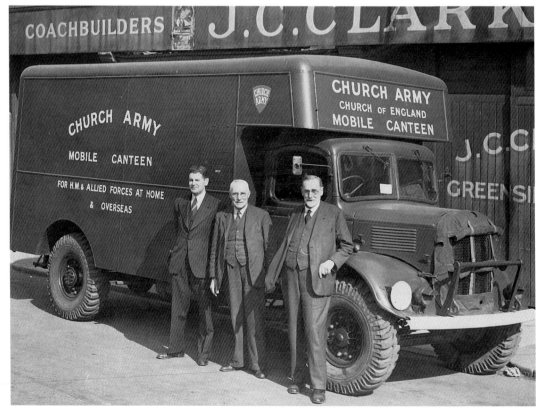

Right: **An Austin K3 with military type tyres and a civilian cab. The mobile canteen body was made for the Church Army by JC Clark.**
(NMM)

This was particularly true of the wireless truck, and to rectify this the C4 Mark II was given a 9ft 0in wheelbase. In 1944 the 4x2 models were replaced by the 4x4 C8/GS which was derived from the FAT (Field Artillery Tractor) described on page 52.

The second company to respond to the War Office specification was Guy Motors of Wolverhampton, which had a long history of making War Office vehicles. Introduced late in 1935, the Guy Ant was similar to the Morris Commercial CS8 in having an angular bonnet with no rounded surfaces and was much the same size, with an 8ft 5in wheelbase and unladen weight of 2 tons 3½cwt. About 90% of its components came from regular production Guy vehicles, including the 3686cc 55bhp Meadows 4ELA engine used in the Otter 6 ton and axles from the Wolf 2-3 ton lorry. As with the Morris Commercial, the original Ants had simple open cabs with twin folding screens for the driver and passenger and no doors, but by 1941 a more civilised cab with half doors and a full-width windscreen had been adopted. There were also civilian versions of the Ant, particularly tankers for taking water to blitzed districts where mains supplies had been destroyed. These had conventional cabs with full-height doors and fitted side windows.

Apart from the GS truck, the Ant was supplied as a compressor unit and wireless van. In 1944 it was superseded by a 4x4 version known as the Quad Ant. This was derived from the Guy artillery tractor which had been made since early 1938, and was the first British four-wheel-drive vehicle in the 15cwt GS class, though it was joined later in the year by the Morris Commercial C8/GS. Like the Ant, it had a canvas cab top and tilt covered body, but was somewhat roomier, with an interior width of 6ft 7ins, compared with 5ft 10ins. Both Ant and QuadAnt had an unusual gear change, confusing to the uninitiated, in which third or top were to the left of first and second. Fewer Ants and Quad Ants were made than Morris Commercials or Bedfords, simply because Guy was a relatively small company. From 1938 to 1941 the factory was completely given over to production of military vehicles but in the latter year they were allowed to make a limited number of VixAnt 15 cwt lorries for essential civilian work. The total number of Guy vehicles supplied to the services up to 1945 was 13,305 and this included several types other than Ants. Nevertheless the 15cwt Guys saw service in most theatres of the war, in France up to the Dunkirk evacuation, in North Africa, Italy and in France again after the

Above: **Two Fordson WOT2 15cwt trucks, followed by a Morris-Commercial CS8, with the 31st Highland Division moving up for an attack in Northern France in February 1945. Just visible behind the trucks is a Studebaker Weasel tracked cargo carrier.** *(IWM)*

Above: **A Bedford OYD disembarking from a LST (Landing Ship, Tanks) during a training exercise.**
(*The Tank Museum, Bovington*)

Right: **A classic Bedford OYD fording a river, followed by a Fordson WOT2. The motorcycle is a Matchless G3L 35M, of which more than 63,000 were made for the army between 1941 and 1945.**
(*NMM*)

Normandy landings. Some Quad Ants were also supplied to Egypt before the war and surplus British Army vehicles were later sold for use in Denmark after the war.

Vauxhall Motors were somewhat later in the field with their MW 15cwt truck, although they showed interest in military vehicles by entering a 12cwt van and a 2-ton lorry in the 1935 War Department trials in North Wales, the event in which the Morris Commercial CS8 and Guy Ant made their first appearances. It was not until two years later that a proper military Bedford appeared, the WD-1. This had a 3180cc six-cylinder engine as used in civilian commercial vehicles and in the 27hp Big Six passenger car. A large air cleaner was incorporated and as this would not fit under the narrow Bedford bonnet, the famous wide, snub-nose bonnet was evolved which characterised all normal control military Bedfords. This design had the additional advantage of allowing for a larger radiator and it was also the first Bedford – and indeed the first British truck of any make – to have built-in headlamps. The 1938 and subsequent models had a larger six-cylinder engine of 3519cc, which developed 72bhp.

Military orders were not forthcoming straight away, probably because the War Department had enough supplies of GS trucks from Morris Commercial and Guy, but as war became increasingly certain, during 1939, the War Department's Director of Mechanisation was in regular touch with Vauxhall to see how many trucks could be provided if the need arose. He was told that 2,000 could be turned out in six to seven months from the date of order, and the eventual rate of production could be 3,000 per month or more. In fact, only one order for 50 trucks had been placed before the outbreak of war, but before the end of September 1939 the Vauxhall factory was fully stretched to meet orders for 27,000 army vehicles. Of this total 11,000 were for the 15cwt truck, which was now called the MW.

Nearly 66,000 MWs were made in several different models, of which the most important were the following:-

MWD – standard GS truck
MWC – 200-gallon water tanker (made by Thompson of Bilston) with power take-off (PTO)-driven pump.
MWG – anti-aircraft-gun carrier, fitted with 20mm Polsten gun.
MWR – radio truck (FFW or Fitted for Wireless in official army terminology). These had specially screened ignition and a generator driven by the PTO. Army MWRs had open bodies similar to those of the MWD, with seats for three operators, but those for the RAF had enclosed van bodies similar to the Morris Commercial radio vans.
MWT – 2 pounder anti-tank-gun tractor.
MWV – enclosed van.

Similar in outward appearance to the Bedford MW was the Commer 'Beetle', which first appeared in 1939. It was powered by a 3180cc six-cylinder

Above: **A pair of Bedford OYs on a training exercise in England. The War Department number L 206783 on the leading truck puts it in the first production contract, placed in 1940. The great majority of the 72,379 OYs made were general carrying trucks such as this one (OYD), but some were supplied as chassis with cab (OYC) for special bodies by various manufacturers. The best known of these were the tankers (bowsers) for water or fuel, made by Butterfields of Shipley. About 5000 bowsers were made.** *(NMM)*

Top: **This convoy of OYDs was photographed in France at the very end of the war, or possibly in the summer of 1945. They are late models as indicated by the sloping bonnet and louvres. The steel sided bodies were adopted fairly early on in the OY's production run, which lasted from 1940 to 1945.**
(NMM)

Above: **A fuel bowser on a QLC chassis with body and equipment by Zwicky Ltd of Slough. It carried 850 gallons of petrol and 100 gallons of oil, and had a Stewart Turner auxiliary engine for pumping.**
(NMM)

engine as used in the company's Superpoise commercial vehicles, and was made only as a 15cwt GS truck. Production was limited and was discontinued before the end of 1939 so that Commer could concentrate on making the 30cwt Q2 and 3-ton Q4 trucks which were based on their civilian designs.

The last 15cwt GS truck to be made in quantity was the Fordson WOT2, which appeared in 1940. It was powered by the familiar 3.6-litre V8 engine, and used the simple bonnet and radiator of other military Fords such as the WOA2 staff cars and WOT3 30cwt trucks. On the first models the cab was a simple affair with canvas top and doors, and individual windscreens, but as with other vehicles in its class it became more civilised with the passage of time, with proper doors, windscreen and sidescreens. It was not the easiest of trucks to drive, because the semi-forward driving position meant that the driver's and passengers' legs had to be accommodated in narrow tunnels between the engine and wheel arches. On the driver's side, the tunnel was not wide enough to take three pedals so the accelerator had to be mounted behind the off-side-wheel arch. This meant that the driver, to operate it, had to keep his right knee bent up towards his chest. The WOT2 was seen mainly as a straightforward GS truck, but a number were supplied as fire appliances to the National Fire Service. There was no 4x4 version of this truck.

There were no other production models built

to the War Office 15cwt specification, but two prototypes were made. The more conventional was the Austin K7 which was powered by the company's 3.5-litre six-cylinder engine and used four-wheel drive, and was designed for easy loading into aircraft. The design incorporated a 2-ton winch.

Much less conventional was the Humber Hexonaut which was a 6x6 truck powered by two Hillman Fourteen engines, each driving three wheels on one side. The wheels were evenly spaced along the chassis, with no conventional steering arrangements - instead the wheels on one side or the other were braked to provide skid steering, as in a tank. The Hexonaut was designed to float and could be carried in a Dakota aircraft, but it is unlikely that such radical design would have been practical in battle conditions. Apart from anything else, the maintenance of two engines per vehicle would have made heavy demands on mechanics' time. Three prototypes of the Hexonaut were made, and one was sold into civilian use, working as a timber tractor in the West Country up to the mid-1950s. It has been rescued and restored for display at the Victory Memorial Museum.

Another 15cwt truck which was still in service at the outbreak of the war, although not built to the War Office specification, was the Austin BYD. This used the chassis of the familiar London taxicab powered by the 1861cc Twelve-Four engine which first saw the light of day in 1921, and had been used in taxicabs since 1930. The bonnet, radiator, mudguards and artillery wheels were straight off the

1937/39 model taxi, known by drivers as the 'Flash Job' because it was marginally more streamlined and modern than its traditional 'square-rigged' predecessors. About 400 chassis which had been intended for cab work were fitted with truck bodies and diverted to the army, who used them for general duties and particularly driving instruction. After the war, about 300 were repurchased by Mann & Overton, the London taxicab distributors, and dismantled for spares to keep the Capital's ageing cab fleet on the road.

Trucks, 30cwt to 4 tons

The official army designation for the 15cwt vehicles just described was 'Truck, 15cwt, 4x2 GS' while 3 tons and up were called by the older name 'Lorry, 3 ton, 4x2 GS', but as the word truck has become so widespread over the past thirty years, it will be used for all load carriers, light or heavy.

The 30 to 40cwt class was a popular one between the wars, and considerable numbers of these trucks were still in service in 1939. They ranged from modified civilian vehicles by Bedford, Morris Commercial and Thornycroft to the Bedford OXD, a larger wheelbase version of the MW, and the Fordson WOT8, which was derived from the 3-ton WOT6, and was the only British four-wheel-drive truck in the 30cwt category. At the outbreak of war the army had more than 10,000 30cwts but over half of these were lost after the

evacuation of Dunkirk. Rather than replace them the army standardised the 3-ton truck, which was often a similar vehicle but with twin rear tyres and sometimes a longer wheelbase.

During the 1930s a number of 30cwt six-wheelers had been made, by Crossley, Garner, Morris Commercial, Thornycroft and Vulcan; of these the Morris Commercial was made in the largest numbers and for the longest period, 1933 to 1944. They came in normal control (CD) and forward control (CDF) versions, and although designed by Morris Commercial they were largely made by Austin (6,686) and Wolseley (nearly 6,000). Variants were the CDFW with winch and the CDSW breakdown truck which was also used as a tractor for the 40mm Bofors AA gun.

The 3-ton truck was very widely used by all the armed services and was the heaviest type that could be made in large numbers. At the start of the war a little under 10,000 were in use, but six years later the figure had risen to 390,000. Not all these were British made, as many thousands were provided by the United States and Canada. The British motor industry made three basic types, the 4x2, mostly normal control and based on civilian designs, the 4x4, which were specialised forward control models, and the 6x4 made with both driver positions.

The most common 4x2s were the Austin K3, Bedford OY and Commer Q4. The Austin was based on the civilian machine with which the Birmingham company had returned to truck manufacture in 1939, after many years of making only

cars, light vans and taxicabs. It was a straightforward design with a 3.5-litre six-cylinder overhead-valve engine, a four-speed constant-mesh gearbox and hydraulic brakes. The military version had an open cab and twin 3.4 x17 rear tyres on the early models, later versions having a slit top closed cab and single 10.50x16 tyres. A shorter-wheelbase version was the K30, a 30cwt truck, and this was also the basis for the K2 ambulance, possibly the most famous Austin product of World War Two (see page 46).

The Bedford OY was the most numerous of all the military vehicles from Luton, being made between 1939 and 1945. Mechanically it was similar to the OL civilian models, but featured the wide, snub-nosed bonnet of the MW, which was both cheaper to make and sturdier than the pointed grille of the OL. The standard GS truck was the OYD and variants included the OYC tanker for both water and petrol (also used as the basis for a canteen van) and the OWL made for essential civilian work, though the latter was rated for 5 ton loads.

The Rootes Group's offering in this class was the Commer Q4, a 3-ton truck closely based on the company's civilian Superpoise model which had been put into production in 1939. Like its contemporaries the first military Q4s had twin 3.4 x17 rear tyres, similar to those on the civilian models, but these were soon replaced by large section single 10.50x16s all round.

There were numerous other 3-ton trucks in the 4x2 class, mostly very similar to civilian models. These included the Albion KL forward control, Dennis 'Pig', Dodge 82, Leyland Lynx, and normal and forward control Thornycrofts. An unusual

Right: **The only QL to be produced with a soft-top cab was a special QLC designed to carry a 6 pound anti-tank gun. They were intended for desert use, and when the North African campaign was completed, they were reworked and fitted with GS bodies, as here.** *(NMM)*

design was the Tilling-Stevens petrol-electric, with a 24kW generator ahead of the engine. This source of electricity was very useful for powering a mobile workshop and also for a searchlight. This made the Tilling-Stevens a popular vehicle with fairground operators when the war was over, providing power and light for roundabouts and sideshows. On the Tilling-Stevens the generator was an integral part of the transmission, but some other trucks such as the Thornycroft ZS/TC4 carried generators whose sole function was to provide power for a searchlight. This was a 90cm projector carried on four very small tracked bogies, and trained onto the target by a handwheel. Most 4x2s were used for general carrying duties including personnel, but there were also some special applications such as communications and mobile X-ray vans.

3 tons, 4x4

Four-wheel drive had received very little attention in Britain during the inter-war years, in contrast to America, which had a tradition of making 4x4 trucks dating back to the early days of World War One. There F.W.D and Jeffery had built more than 55,000 such trucks, mostly during the war years, and the F.W.D Corporation continued in production with 4x4s and later 6x6s right up to the outbreak of World War Two, so they were in an excellent position to go into large-scale manufacture of their SU-COE 3-ton truck as soon as hostilities began. In fact quite a number were supplied to the British Army under 'lend-lease' before

America itself entered the war. By contrast, Britain had no commercial manufacturer of four-wheel-drive vehicles, although a few prototypes had been built by Commer, Karrier, Guy and Garner, the latter to the designs of the talented Hungarian Nicholas Straussler. Some of these took part in War Department trials in North Wales during October 1938, and it was probably this event which sparked off interest in four-wheel drive among Vauxhall's engineering department. They were already in regular consultation with the War Office about military vehicles and were soon to go into production with the Bedford MW 15cwt truck. It was at a meeting on 23 December 1938 that Vauxhall first suggested the idea of a 4x4 truck to the War Office and received a favourable answer, though no orders were placed.

Design work began, but there was no urgency, and Vauxhall were still almost entirely orientated towards civilian work. Then on 12 September 1939, nine days after the outbreak of war, War Office officials went to the factory with a request for Vauxhall to proceed with prototype work on the 4x4. Two weeks later, by which time raw materials could only be obtained against a Government permit, Vauxhall were given authorisation to obtain any material necessary for building the prototypes. On 16 November, the company's Chief Engineer circulated a memo saying "No work of any description is to be allowed to interfere with the carrying out of all work necessary in the development of the 4x4 vehicle".

On 1 February 1940 the first prototype was ready, and within a month two more were delivered

to the Army who put them through strenuous trials before placing an order for an initial batch of 4,272 trucks. The new model was given the designation QL, no one quite knows why, but probably the 'Q' stood for Quad, a common name for 4x4s, and 'L' for Long, as it was a full-length truck and not an artillery tractor.

The newcomer was very different from anything else that had emerged from the Luton factory since production of Bedford trucks had begun there in 1931. Apart from its four-wheel drive, it was considerably larger in appearance than any previous Bedford, and the first to have full forward control. The engine was the standard $3\frac{1}{2}$-litre six-cylinder petrol unit which had powered thousands of civilian Bedfords as well as the 4x2 3-ton OY military truck. Vauxhall engineers were not happy

about this, and would have liked something more powerful, but to have developed a bigger engine would have wasted precious time and there was also the desperate need for standardisation. Four-wheel drive was not permanently engaged, so that on good metalled roads the QL could operate as a 4x2, thus saving on fuel consumption and tyre wear. When the time came for off-road work, the driver could engage drive to the front wheels by moving a lever which at the same time engaged the low ratio in the two-speed transfer box. It then had remarkable pulling power, being able to keep going through mud as deep as the wheels. Drivers found that the tyres seemed to have the effect of paddle wheels, so long as the revs were kept down.

The gearbox was a four-speed unit, and final drive on both axles was by spiral bevel. Gross vehicle weight was 6 tons 17cwt in standard form, and payload in the region of 3 tons.

Although orders were placed in mid-1940, it was not until February 1941 that the first production QLs went into service. For one thing, manufacture of the conventional OY and smaller Bedfords had to be maintained at a high level to make up for the loss of more than three quarters of the army's vehicles after the evacuation at Dunkirk. Also the introduction of a 4x4 design into factories already producing 4x2s was not without its problems. The plant was geared up to make one engine, one gearbox and one driving axle per vehicle and the need for an additional drive axle doubled the demand for machining facilities, not to mention the extra gear-cutting needed to make the transfer boxes. Apart from the extra machinery required, it took 30% more manpower to build a 4x4 than a

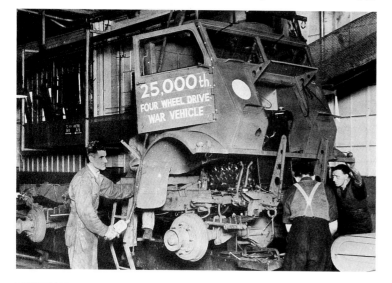

4x2 and manpower was an uncertain factor at Vauxhall as in all other truck factories, with the increasing demands for servicemen and transfer of labour to other industries with higher priority. Despite these problems, a total of 52,245 QLs were built between 1941 and 1945, making them by far the most common of Britain's military vehicles in the 4x4 3 ton class.

Strictly speaking, there was no such truck as a Bedford QL; they all bore suffixes to indicate particular applications and these are listed below in alphabetical order:

QLB – tractor for 40mm Bofors AA gun. Special body for carrying crew of eight men plus driver, two in cab, five in crew compartment amidships and two in rear section. This section also carried ammunition cases, kit containers, etc. Equipment included 5-ton winch driven from a PTO.

QLC – truck/tractor with semi-trailer. Small cargo body of 1 ton capacity behind cab, 6-ton semi-trailer attached permanently by Tasker ball-type coupling.

Unlike many tractors, the QLC used the same wheelbase as the trucks, making it seem abnormally long for a tractor, though the small cargo body made effective use of the space between cab and trailer coupling. Trailers were made by Glover, Webb & Liversidge or Scottish Motor Traction to a common design.

QLD – standard 3-ton cargo truck with open body and detachable tarpaulin. Special versions of the QLD included office and battery storage trucks, workshops and kitchens. Nearly 1,500 of the latter were made, from late 1943 onwards.

QLR – wireless truck with house type body and canvas tent extension. This 'signals wagon' was the longest lived of the QLs and some remained in service until the early 1970s. The bodies were made by the car builder Lagonda, and by coachbuilders such as Duple, Mulliner and Tickford.

QLT – troop carrier, nicknamed 'the Drooper' because their additional rear overhang made them tail heavy. With their full load of 29 men plus their equipment, weight distribution was satisfactory but if a smaller party of men chose to sit at the back (and they frequently did), handling became distinctly alarming. The bodies and chassis modifications for the QLT were in fact made at the Austin factory, and a total of 3,373 QLTs were made, from August 1941 to the end of the war.

QLW – winch equipped tipper with three cubic yard Edbro tipping body. About 1,000 were made, of which the last 600 were designed to be dismantled and carried in two Dakota aircraft. (QLW, APT – Air Portable Truck). The chassis without wheels and axles, together with the lower half of the cab, went in one aircraft and the body (split transversely), cab top, wheels and winch in the other.

There were also numerous other special vehicles built on the QL chassis, including fire engines, mobile workshops, kitchens, dental surgeries, fuel tankers and an armoured flame-thrower. Two experimental derivations were the Bedford Bren which used the tracked-drive of a Bren-gun carrier in place of the rear wheels, and the Giraffe, with raised cab and engine – for wading through the sea. The transfer box remained at chassis level, drive being taken to it by enclosed chain. The engine was seven feet above the ground and the driver more than ten feet. The design did not go into production as by 1944, when it would have been needed,

Vauxhall engineers had developed a satisfactory method of waterproofing standard trucks.

Many QLs were used for civilian purposes after the war, particularly as timber tractors and breakdown trucks. An unusual application was made by Southport Corporation, in North West England, who fitted several with open bus bodies and used them for a seafront passenger service along the beach. The QL was extremely important for General Motors as the lessons learnt in its design and operation were applied in its successors, the RL, M and TM 4x4 Bedford trucks.

No other British 4x4 truck was made in the same quantity as the QL, but there were several important contributions to the war effort from other manufacturers, in particular Ford and Austin.

The Fordson WOT6 followed the QL pattern in using a familiar engine, in this case the 85bhp side-valve Ford V8 used in other WOT models. Like the QL, the Fordson had a newly designed forward-control cab of angular aspect, and final drive through a four-speed gearbox and two-speed transfer box. Like the later production QLs, the cab roof was detachable to reduce shipping height. Most WOT6s were fitted with conventional drop-side cargo bodies and there was not the variety of bodywork that was seen on the Bedford. However there were some specials, including a compressor lorry which was fitted with a petrol-driven Reavell

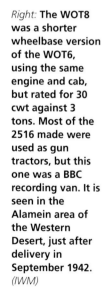

Right: **The WOT8 was a shorter wheelbase version of the WOT6, using the same engine and cab, but rated for 30 cwt against 3 tons. Most of the 2516 made were used as gun tractors, but this one was a BBC recording van. It is seen in the Alamein area of the Western Desert, just after delivery in September 1942.** *(IWM)*

Left: **A Humber heavy utility restored by a Guernsey enthusiast. About 6500 of these 4x4s were made in all forms.**
(Nick Georgano)

Below: **The Humber heavy utility was one of the most promising British vehicles developed during the war. Powered by the familiar 4086cc engine used in pre-war Super Snipe cars, it had comfortable seating for seven and a good cross-country performance. In concept it was an ancestor of today's Range Rover type of vehicle.**
(Vehicle displayed at the Victory Memorial Museum)

Above: **A Willys Jeep with anti-aircraft machine guns front and rear. These were fitted in England for special use by the SAS.**
(John Blackman)

Right: **A standard Bedford MWD 15cwt truck. Nearly 66,000 MWs were made in many different versions.**
(John Blackman)

Above: **An AEC Matador 4x4 heavy truck with an Austin K2 ambulance parked alongside.**
(John Blackman)

Centre: **The Austin K5 3-ton 4x4 was the Birmingham company's answer to the Bedford QL.**
(The Tank Museum, Bovington)

Left: **Morris-Commercial C4 15cwt GS truck.**
(John Blackman)

Right: **The Bedford OY in its standard form, when it was known as the OYD. The earliest models had 32x6 dual tyres, but the great majority were fitted with 10.50-16 singles.** *(John Blackman)*

Below: **The Bedford QL was the most widespread British-made 4x4 in World War Two, with a total of 52,247 delivered between 1941 and 1945. Many saw service with the British Army well into the 1950s in Aden, Cyprus, Korea and Malaya. This is a standard QLD cargo truck for 3 ton loads.**

Left: **The best known British ambulance of World War Two was the Austin K2, which repaced the other designs from 1940 onwards. More than 13,000 were made. This restored example was discovered in a scrap dealer's yard in Oxfordshire; the owner not only rebuilt it but gradually acquired all the necessary equipment such as stretchers and first aid kit.**
(J Spencer-Smith)

Left: **This Ford-built CMP 3-tonner is an F60S (F=Ford, 60cwt S=short wheelbase). The wheelbase was 134 inches, compared with 158 inches for the F60L.**
(The Tank Museum, Bovington)

Right: **The later-type of Standard 'Tilly' with military-style grille. It wears the camouflage and numbering of the HQ, 11th Armoured Division, North West Europe.**
(Vehicle displayed at the Victory Memorial Museum)

Right: **The Leyland Hippo was one of the Army's 10-ton 6x4 trucks, the largest category of rigid chassis used by the British Army in World War Two. This is the Mark II, introduced in 1944 and made for several years after the war. Its 7.4-litre six-cylinder diesel engine developed 100bhp, and drove through a five-speed gearbox.**
(The Tank Museum, Bovington)

compressor mounted transversely at the front and feeding four high-pressure compressed-air storage cylinders. Production of the WOT6 ran from January 1942 until September 1945 and the total made was nearly 30,000. There was also a shorter version known as the WOT8, rated at 30cwt and used as a tractor for the 17 pounder anti-tank gun, as well as for general duties. Just over 2500 of these were manufactured.

Austin's contribution to the 4x4 3-ton series was designated K5. It too had a well tried engine, the 85bhp six-cylinder unit used in the new range of Austin commercial trucks introduced shortly before the outbreak of war. This overhead-valve engine (Austin's first) was also used in the post-war Sheerline and Princess cars. The K5 was equipped with servo-assisted hydraulic brakes. Quite a number were made with soft-top cabs or half cabs, and there was a version for anti-tank work with a six pounder gun mounted on the truck's platform and firing forward over the open cab. This version had a gun blast shield over the radiator. Total production of the K5, introduced into service in 1941, was 12,280.

Several other manufacturers built 4x4 3-ton trucks in smaller numbers than the Bedford or Austin. These included Albion, whose FT11 was made from February 1940 to August 1944, Karrier, whose K6 had been developed before the war and went into production in December 1940, Crossley, whose Q2 was built for the RAF, and Thornycroft, who built about 5,000 Nubians from June 1940 onwards. The Nubian was in fact the only one of these 4x4s which were brought into being by the

War to continue in production well after 1945. In 4x4 and 6x6 forms the Nubian was made up to the early 1970s, and the name survived on the rear-engined fire engines made by Scammell up to the 1980s. The wartime Nubian was available with a 5.2-litre 85bhp petrol engine or 5.25-litre 61bhp diesel unit. Final drive was by epicyclic gearing in the wheel hubs.

3 tons, 6x4

The 'Rigid Six' three-axle truck was a popular type between the wars, and with a tandem-drive rear bogie, or 6x4 layout, was favoured by the Army, as it combined reasonable cross-country performance with good load carrying capacity. A variety of 6x4s in 30cwt and 3 ton models were made by Albion, Crossley, Garner, Guy, Karrier, Leyland, Morris Commercial, Thornycroft and Vulcan. A number of these were still in use at the outbreak of War, and they were joined by new types for which large orders were placed. The 4x4 truck was seen as the preferable design in the long run, but with none available immediately the 6x4 was called on for a variety of duties.

There were three main types of 6x4 built from 1939 to 1945, the Austin K3 and 6, Fordson WOT1 and Leyland Retriever, with other types being supplied by AEC, Albion and Thornycroft.

The first six-wheeled Austin was the K3, powered by the 3.9-litre six-cylinder engine used in other Austin commercials, with a 12ft 9in wheelbase and weight of 4 tons 8cwt. Early models had open cabs but all K3s retained the civilian-type bonnet and radiator as used on the K2 ambulance

Top: **The Leyland Hippo II 10-ton 6x4 was introduced in 1944 and was distinguished from the Hippo 1 by its closed cab and more powerful, though smaller, engine.** *(Peter Daniels/NMM)*

Above: **A restored Dennis Max II with signals van body.** *(Nick Georgano)*

Right: **A Dennis Max II with military-type cab in civilian use as a fuel tanker for the Pool Board.** *(Nick Baldwin Collection)*

and K3 4x2 trucks. In 1942 the K3 was superseded by the K6 which was generally similar but could be immediately distinguished by its more utilitarian front end. The K6 was mainly used by the RAF with the following bodies:-

AIR TRAFFIC CONTROL: house-type body with all necessary equipment for flying control in remote sites or on airfields where the existing equipment had been destroyed by enemy action. It had large side windows, and also an observation glass-house, known as a Belvedere, which contained a revolving seat for the airfield controller.

BALLOON WINCH: this operated barrage balloons, the winch being powered by a Ford V8 industrial engine mounted in the centre of the body. The winch mechanism and operator's cabin were protected from fouling by the handling lines by wire mesh, and by a tarpaulin cover in bad weather. Similar bodies were mounted on the Fordson WOT1. At first the winch trucks were kept at fixed sites, but particularly after the deployment of V-1 flying bombs in 1944 they needed to be moved rapidly around the Home Counties. After the war a few barrage balloons were used for the parachute training of airborne troops, so some winch trucks remained in service, replaced by a Leyland in the 1970s and a Bedford in the 1980s.

BOMB CARRIER: a simple platform body with hinged chock rails along the side.

BUS: a 23 passenger van-type vehicle, used mainly to transport aircrew to distant parts of aerodromes in all weathers. They had double doors at the rear and an emergency exit on each side between the windows.

CRANE: Coles EMA Mark VI Series 2 cranes, with a lifting capacity of 3 tons, were fitted to a number of K6 chassis.

FIRE-CRASH TENDER: equipped with carbon dioxide cylinders in four banks of six and also two wheel-mounted extinguishers, searchlight and fog lamp. Although ordered during the war this equipment was not delivered on the K6 chassis until 1946.

GENERAL SERVICE AND STORES: some were fitted with fixed lockers and storage bins, others with simple canvas-topped bodies and clear floor space. The K6 was the only British truck to carry its spare wheel in a locker at the front end of the body, although this was quite common on Australian-made vehicles.

MOBILE OFFICES: which could also be used as laboratories, recruiting stations or signals trucks. These vehicles

were often used in pairs or threes, with awnings joining them together to give substantial accommodation.

POWER AND CHARGING UNITS: equipped with a Tangye VCR2 or Lister JP4 diesel engine driving a 230v generator. These were used not only for powering equipment but for charging batteries. The latter might be a truck's own or large banks of batteries used to charge those of tanks in the field. These would be carried up to the tanks by Loyd tracked carriers.

TIPPERS: fitted with Edbro 2EL power-operated hydraulic tipping gear, and used mainly for the construction and repair of airfields.

In addition to these RAF applications, the K6 was used by the army as a breakdown truck, with a 5-ton winch and 10½cwt of pig-iron ballast at the front to compensate for the extra load at the rear. They were also used in conjunction with a six-wheeled recovery trailer. These breakdown trucks became popular with garages after the war, while two K6 mobile offices were used by Billy Smart's Circus until well into the 1960s.

Two types of Fordson 6x4 were used by the armed forces, the E917T which was basically a civilian design, and the WOT1. Both used the

Above: **Another popular chassis for crane carrying was the Thornycroft Amazon, which, like the AEC, used a Coles Mark VII. About 2000 were made during the war, of which the RAF took 1800.**
(NMM)

Left: **Austin K6 with Coles EMA Mark VI crane. The RAF used a few of these, but preferred the AEC 854 or Thornycroft Amazon with greater lifting capacity.**
(IWM)

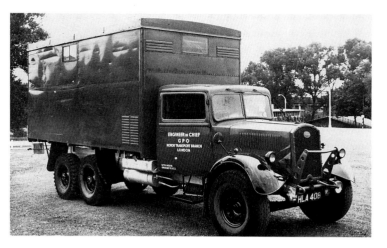

familiar 85bhp V8 engine. The E917T had the oval radiator grille of the American-style trucks and a 6x4 conversion by County Commercial Cars Ltd of Fleet, Hampshire, as Ford themselves did not make a six-wheeled chassis at this time. The civilian 6x4 was known as the Sussex and the 6x2 model as the Surrey. Several different bodies were mounted on the E917T (and its 1938 model predecessor, the E817T) including a barrage balloon winch similar to that used on the Austin K6.

The WOT1 was similar in general layout, but had a military-style bonnet and cab similar to that used on the 30cwt WOT3 and a larger wheelbase of 13ft 8½ in compared with the E917's 13ft 1in. The later WOT1A had a 14ft 10in wheelbase, while the WOT1A/1 was similar but with servo-assisted

braking. Several of the bodies on the WOT1 were similar to those on the Austin K6, including the bus, fire tender, balloon winch, power unit, general service and signals vehicles. Fire tenders were available with foam and/or carbon dioxide and, unlike the Austin, were used from 1942 onwards. Uses peculiar to the Fordson were ambulance, dental laboratory, dental surgery and parachute drying van. The latter contained two electric fans each with six 500-watt heaters, and could dry three parachutes at a time. When the air temperature reached 100°F, fresh cold air was admitted through thermostatically controlled louvres, and the hot damp air expelled via an exhauster on the front bulkhead. When the van was full of cold air the heaters and fans came on automatically and the cycle continued until the parachutes were dry. The 230v power supply came from an outside source.

The Leyland Retriever was an older design, dating from the mid-1930s and the first series of 6x4 army trucks. It differed from the Austin and Fordson in having forward control and a larger four-cylinder engine of 5.9-litres, though developing about the same power at 73bhp. Nearly all Retrievers had open cabs, with folding canvas roofs, later ones having full windscreens. Among the bodies available on the Retriever chassis were a breakdown truck, general service, Coles crane, searchlight and camera/darkroom/photo-mechanical. The latter involved three trucks parked side by side which provided a full photographic developing and printing service. This work was later

performed by larger vehicles such as the 10-ton Leyland Hippo and Foden DG6. Other specialised bodies on the Retriever included types for carrying folding boats and a pontoon carrier for two bow or centre pontoons of a Bailey bridge. These were especially valuable during the Eighth Army's Italian campaign when they were advancing over terrain slotted by narrow valleys and fast flowing rivers. A total of 6,542 Retrievers were made from 1933 to 1944 and some of them remained in Army service until the mid-1960s.

Other trucks in the same category as the Retriever were the AEC Marshal, of which 600 were made, Albion BY, Crossley IGL8, Karrier CK6, Guy FBAX and Thornycroft Tartar. They were all basically 1930s designs, with open cabs; some such as the Crossley were phased out early on in the war, while the Albion BY5 was made up to August 1945. Apart from a few of the later Thornycroft Tartars, which were diesel powered, all used petrol engines.

5 to 10 tons, 4x2 & 6x4

The heavier trucks were all based on pre-war commercial designs, and were mostly powered by diesel engines. Exceptions were the Commer Superpoise Q6, Dennis 5 ton and Fordson Thames 7V. The 5- to 6-ton trucks were 4x2s and the larger models 6x4s. The four-wheelers usually wore the same tyres as their civilian counterparts, with dual wheels at the rear, so were not suitable for desert work or anywhere away from metalled roads. However, they came into their own after the Normandy landings, covering the increasingly long hauls between the beachheads and the forward supply dumps. A division and its supporting troops needed about 520 tons of supplies per day and with 18 divisions engaged on the Western Front, it can be seen that the greater loads that could be carried in one truck the better. Among the British models used were the

Foden DG4/6, E.R.F 2C14, Maudsley Militant and Dennis Max. The latter used a military cab in its Mark II version, but most trucks in this class were little changed from civilian models.

The 6x4 10-ton trucks had either large section single tyres all round (Albion CX23 and Foden DG6/12) or twin rears (Albion CX6N, Leyland Hippo). They were used mainly with camera/darkroom/photo-mechanical bodies similar to those on the Leyland Retriever, though with considerably more space. The bodies could be extended at the sides and rear when the vehicle was stationary. Other special bodies on the Foden included a heavy coastal gun used in conjunction with an armoured half-cab. The Fodens and Leyland Hippos remained in service for many years after the war, the latter being developed into the Hippo Mark III or 19H/1.

Ambulances

As with other types of vehicle, the army's fleet of ambulances at the outbreak of war was a very mixed bag. About 20% of the 1,700 machines were impressed vehicles, some of them not suitable for transporting the fit, let alone the sick. Elizabeth Nagle-Turnbull, then a 20-year old FANY (First Aid Nursing Yeomanry) driver, remembers an ancient Albion coal-truck, with a leaking exhaust and innocent of front-wheel brakes or electric starter, which she had to deliver from Shorncliffe to Dover, in company with a hardly more salubrious Commer laundry van. Much more comfortable was the Morris Commercial CS11/30F, based on the civilian 30cwt chassis and supplied to the army in considerable numbers between 1935 and 1939. The four-stretcher bodies were made by Mann Egerton, and had a canvas topped cab. The exhaust pipe was fitted vertically between just behind the cab and the main body. These ambulances were often presented by private individuals or organisations.

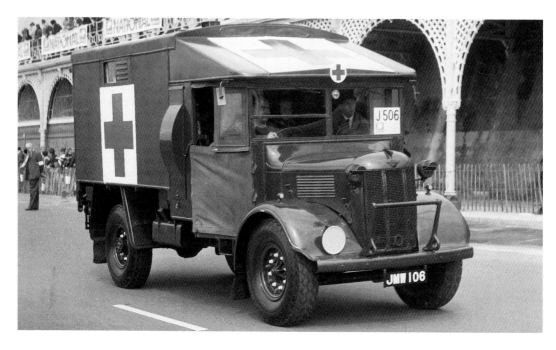

A smaller vehicle which was also widely used as an ambulance was the Morris TMV 10cwt semi-forward-control van. This had a proper enclosed cab and doors, but the body was very functional and fitted with only the bare necessities. However, like the larger Morris Commercial, it could carry four stretchers, or eight sitting patients. It was used by the Home Guard as well as the Army.

The ambulances described so far were used for non-operational work in the United Kingdom, rather than on the battlefield. For evacuation of the wounded from the immediate battle area, the most widely used vehicle was the Jeep, which, amazingly, could be equipped to carry four stretchers, though three were more common. The Humber 4x4 was also used, carrying two stretchers, and this gave much better weather protection to both crew and patients. The best known British ambulance of the war was the Austin K2, familiarly known as the 'Katie'. This used the same chassis as the K3, 30cwt truck (see page 28). The Mann-Egerton-built body was wood framed, leather cloth covered, and designed to carry four stretchers to a standard War Office specification, which was also used on the Morris Commercial CS11/30F and Bedford ML chassis. From 1940 onwards the K2 became the

standard army ambulance and the other types were discontinued. A total of 13,102, K2s were manufactured under ten contracts covering the period from August 1939 to June 1945, and were supplied to a number of other countries such as France, Norway and the Soviet Union.

A number fell into German hands after the evacuation at Dunkirk. At least one of these saw service on the Russian front, then transferred to France after the D-Day landings, to be recaptured by the British in August 1944. Field Marshal Montgomery, Commander of the 21st Army Group which made the capture, sent the ambulance back to its makers at Longbridge.

The K2 was also used by the American forces, to whom it was supplied under 'reverse lend-lease'. The Americans found it superior to any of their own makes, thanks to its combination of comfort, good ground clearance and low centre of gravity which enabled it to reach spots inaccessible by other ambulances. The K2 remained in British Army and Navy service for over ten years after the war, receiving proper doors and cab in the post-war years. Surplus military ambulances were sold to France, Belgium and the Netherlands.

The standard RAF ambulance was the Fordson WOT1, 6x4, but this large vehicle was not easy to manoeuvre in country lanes, and was replaced by the K2 for the Normandy campaign.

Tractor/Trailer Units

The British Army did not make widespread use of truck tractors, and those that were employed were often of American or Canadian manufacture, such as Autocar, Brockway, FWD, International, Mack or Studebaker.

Of British made tractors, the Bedford OXC (short-wheelbase MW) was the most common, used in conjunction with a Scammell semi-trailer with automatic coupling. These had either GS dropsided bodies or petrol tankers. The Bedford OXC was also used as a tractor with the 40ft low-loading trailer familiarly known as the 'Queen Mary', after the famous passenger liner. These trailers, made of arc-welded, rolled steel sections, had a well-type body and hinged tailboard/ramp. The inside of the body, floor and tailboard were lined with timber. The two wheels were suspended independently by coil springs and 10.50x20 tyres were fitted. The trailer was 40ft long by 12ft 3in wide

Above: **An Albion ambulance for the RAF on the AM463 chassis, which was also used for refuelling and crane-trucks.** *(Bart Vanderveen Collection)*

Below: **Bedford OXC with a Taskers 'Queen Mary' 40 foot trailer carrying a damaged Spitfire. Behind it is an AEC Matador 4x4 artillery tractor.** *(NMM)*

and the overall length of the whole vehicle 50ft or more, depending on the tractor.

All 'Queen Marys' were made by the well known trailer manufacturers Taskers of Andover, Hampshire, who supplied a total of 3,837 to the Navy and RAF. They were used for carrying complete body or wing sections of aircraft. The body of a Wellington bomber was 64ft 7in long so even on a 'Queen Mary' one end projected beyond the trailer while the other extended over the tractor's cab. The Lancaster, at 69ft 4in, was too large to be transported whole, so its fuselage was divided just behind the cockpit.

As well as the Bedford OXC, tractors used by the RAF included the Commer Q2 and the 4x4 Crossley Q-type. These were both forward-control designs, giving shorter overall length than the Bedford. Despite its size, the original 'Queen Mary' was only rated for a 3 ton load, but in October 1943 there came a new 5-ton model. It was no longer than its predecessor, but was six inches wider. This was designed to be used in conjunction with the newly introduced Crossley Q-type, but it was perfectly suitable for towing by Bedford or Commer tractors. The Crossley could also be used in conjunction with full trailers, in which case a 2-ton ballast box was carried behind the cab. The author encountered one of these in London in 1968, towing tar spreading equipment.

Tank Transporters

During World War One the British Army had no truck transporters for tanks, which were all taken

Above: **This Scammell Pioneer is bringing a damaged M4 Sherman tank to a REME field workshop in Germany prior to the crossing of the Rhine in early 1945. These workshops moved from one dump of damaged vehicles to another, repairing as many as could be saved.** *(The Tank Museum, Bovington)*

Left: **The Pioneer
had a reputation
for getting out of
almost any tight
spot, and of
rescuing other
vehicles as well.
It is carrying a
Matilda tank on
its 30-ton trailer.**
(The Tank Museum,
Bovington)

by rail as near to the front as possible, and then driven off to the battlefront. In 1927, Scammell introduced their Pioneer 6x4 tractor which was adapted to pull a semi-trailer carrying a Vickers Mark II Medium tank. The two-axle bogie on the trailer was detachable to allow the tank to be driven up on to it, but in 1939 this arrangement was replaced by a fixed bogie with hinged loading ramps, which made for much quicker loading. Despite steady progress during the 1930s by Scammell's design department, the army did not place any serious orders, and at the outbreak of war only two Pioneer tank transporters were in service. Further orders were immediately placed, but the Pioneer was also made as a heavy artillery tractor, and as this had priority, tank transporters were always in short supply. A total of 548 Pioneers were made in six years, and the shortfall was made up by the Albion CX24 and, more importantly, by American makes such as Diamond T, Federal and Reo.

The early Pioneers had Scammell's own 7-litre 85bhp four-cylinder petrol engine, but the models made for the Army were powered by Gardner 6LW six-cylinder diesel engines of 8369cc developing 102bhp. They had six forward speeds and one reverse. The pivoted front axle had transverse-leaf independent suspension and the rear axles had rocking balance beams, so that any of the six wheels could rise to a height of six feet without twisting the frame. This suspension system was designed by O.D North who was responsible for the 100-ton Scammell transporter of 1929, and also for the streamlined rear-engined North Lucas car of 1922.

The Pioneer was also equipped with an 8-ton vertical spindle winch.

The 20-ton two-axle trailers were made only by Scammell, but later 30-ton trailers were made by Shelvoke & Drewry as well as Scammell. The S & D trailers were originally designed for use in conjunction with the Diamond T 980 tractor (see page 164), and incorporated counterbalanced loading ramps that could be operated by one man, designed by James Drewry. Shelvoke & Drewry also manufactured 40-ton three-axle drawbar trailers, as did Crane, both being designed to carry a Churchill tank. These trailers were used only with Diamond T tractors.

The Scammell Pioneer was also built as a heavy recovery tractor, for pulling disabled vehicles most of these had a Herbert Morris 2½-ton sliding-jib crane, but a few had collapsible jibs. They could also be fitted with tracks over the rear bogie. A total of about 1,500 recovery tractors were made, compared with 548 tank transporters and 786 artillery tractors.

Because of the shortage of Scammells, and before the Diamond T was available, the army ordered a number of Albion CX24 6x4 tractors. This model was developed from the CX22S heavy artillery tractor, and was powered by a 9080cc 100bhp six-cylinder diesel engine. A total of 800 were made, but they proved to be insufficiently strong for tank hauling, especially in North African conditions and were regulated to transporting cable drums and telegraph poles, for which they were rated at 15 rather than 20 tons.

Bottom left: **This
Pioneer, 'Snow
White', went to
France with the
1st Armoured
Division, and
unlike many other
vehicles, returned
to Britain and had
a further lease of
life in the Western
Desert. It has the
original design of
semi-trailer, in
which the rear
bogies had to be
detached for the
tank to be loaded.**
(The Tank Museum,
Bovington)

Right: **A Morris-Commercial C8 in a warmer climate, with the door fixed open to aid cooling. C8s were used by Canadian and Australian forces in World War Two, and by the Dutch in Java in the late 1940s.**
(The Tank Museum, Bovington)

Centre: **The Pioneer was also used as an artillery tractor, in which form it was known as the R100. They had accomodation for the crew of nine. This one is towing a 6-inch howitzer of 3rd Heavy Battery, Royal Artillery.**
(The Tank Museum, Bovington)

Right: **Introduced in 1938 and made up to 1945, The AEC Matador was Britain's first quantity-built 4x4 heavy truck. This one has just crossed the Elbe in the last stages of the war, 30 April 1945. It was in the service of the 2nd Battalion, Gordon Highlanders, who found the Elbe district very similar to the wooded hills of their native Deeside.**
(IWM)

Perhaps to compensate for the inadequacy of the CX24, Albion built two prototypes of a most unusual tank transporter tractor called the CX33. This was powered by two 140bhp six-cylinder diesel engines mounted side-by-side behind the driver's cab. The tractor had four axles close together, the outer pair being driven by one engine and the inner by the other. Steering was by the front and rear axles. The driver sat in the centre of his wide cab, with crew on either side of him. There was a similar cab at the rear of the vehicle, in which sat the winch crew. The CX33 was capable of pulling 75 tons, nearly twice the weight of a Churchill tank. The first prototype was ready for tests in January 1943 but was never taken up by the Army, presumably because of complexity and cost. A second prototype, in which only three of the four axles drove, and steering was by the front pair, was built in August 1945, but it had no successors.

Artillery Tractors

The need for a tractor to pull field artillery pieces is one of the oldest requirements of any army, and indeed the world's first self-propelled vehicle, the steam tractor built by Nicolas Cugnot in 1770, was intended to tow artillery. The British Army bought their first steam traction engine, an Aveling Steam Sapper, in 1871, and later engines saw service in the Boer War and World War One.

Scammell, Guy and FWD manufactured petrol-engined tractors in the 1930s, and by the outbreak of war a new generation of light 4x4s had entered production, by Guy and Morris Commercial. The Guy Quad Ant appeared in prototype form in late 1937, entering production the following year. It used the same 55bhp Meadows engine as the Ant 15cwt GS truck (see page 21), and had accommodation for a crew of six and 96 rounds of ammunition, tools, etc. The Quad Ant was specifically designed to tow the new 25 pounder Howitzer, and the Morris Commercial C8 was in the same category, having a generally similar all-enclosed body with sloping rear. On the Mark III version of the C8 this was replaced by an open body with canvas tilt, but Guy never reached a similar stage with their Quad Ant. Instead they discontinued their artillery tractor in 1943, replacing it with a 15cwt GS truck which was the first British-built 4x4 to be built in this class.

A similar FAT (Field Artillery Tractor) was made by Karrier, their KT4 based on the Humber armoured car chassis, but with the 4-litre six-cylinder engine moved to the front. The body was made by BLSP (British Light Steel Panels) of Slough, Bucks. About 400 of these KT4s were made between September 1939 and January 1940 for the Indian Army, and later saw service with the Indian divisions of the Eighth Army in North Africa and Italy. They were suitable for towing 18 and 25 pounder Howitzers.

Other tractors in this class included the 6x6 Albion FT 15 which only went into production in 1945 and the twin-engined Garner Straussler G3. This was designed by the Hungarian engineer Nicholas Straussler and was built by Garner Motors Ltd of London, NW10. It used two 3.6-litre Ford

Below: **An AEC Matador towing a 3.7 mobile Bofors AA gun on an awkward bend probably in Sicily or Italy judging from the terrain; note spectating peasant with his donkey and summer attire of the crew.** *(The Tank Museum, Bovington)*

Above: **Morris-Commercial C8 artillery tractors taking part in the victory parade of the 51st Highland Division in Bremerhaven on 12 May 1945. The salute was taken by Lt. General Brian Horrocks.** *(IWM)*

Right: **An Austin-built Morris-Commercial C8 with the 61st Division, crossing a pontoon bridge during an exercise in County Antrim in 1942.** *(IWM)*

V8 engines mounted side-by-side under a wide bonnet, with two gearboxes driving a transfer box from which power was taken to front and rear axles. The left-hand engine drove the front axle and the right-hand the rear axle. The engines could be used separately for normal road work and jointly for cross-country travel, but they were not always synchronised, with the result that one worked harder than the other and eventually seized. There were also problems in changing two sets of gears with one lever, but nevertheless 53 Garner Strausslers were made, originally for the Turkish Government, but also used by the British Army in North Africa. Their appearance was much more like a 3-ton GS truck than the other British FATs, and they could also be used as ordinary load carriers.

A different class of tractor was needed for the 40mm Bofors gun or various sizes of Anti-Tank (AT) gun. These included the 6x4 Morris Commercial CD/SW and the 4x4 Morris Commercial C8/AT, both of which had open canvas tilt bodies, and also the Bedford QL and Austin K5. The Bedford could either tow a 40mm Bofors gun or carry a 6 pounder AT gun. As a tractor it was known as the QLB (see page 21), while the AT gun was carried on a normal QLD GS truck. When carried, the AT gun could be fired forward over the cab. The Austin K5 was similar, both trucks having blast shields over their radiators.

Two other trucks which carried guns were the AEC Matador (6 pounder) and Thornycroft Amazon (17 pounder). The bodies of both these vehicles were armoured and the fixed guns mounted on the rear. A total of 175 Matadors were made, but the Amazon was so heavy with its armour and gun (which weighed 6,500 pounds) that its cross-country performance was very disappointing and it was not ordered in quantity.

The AEC Matador was better known as a medium artillery tractor, in which role it was used throughout the war. The first heavy 4x4 truck made in quantity in Britain, the Matador had its origins in the Hardy 4 tonner introduced for the civilian market in 1930. These were made in small numbers, mainly for export, at the AEC factory, and were of similar design and appearance to the 4x2 AEC models, apart from their two-speed auxiliary gearboxes and all-wheel drive. The Matador was introduced late in 1938 and differed from the Hardy chiefly in having a diesel engine, though petrol units were also available. It was officially designated the AEC Forward Model 0853, but this was soon changed to Matador, possibly inspired by its other title, Medium Artillery Tractor. The standard engine was a 7.58-litre six-cylinder diesel developing 95bhp and the petrol option was a 7.41-litre 92bhp unit. The latter were supplied to the RAF in the early years of the war, though they later turned to diesel engines except for the 6x6 Matador-based

fuel tankers. Matadors were also supplied to Norway, but because of the urgency of the Norwegian order a number of diesel Matador chassis intended for other areas of the war had to be hastily converted to petrol, all to little avail as they were lost with the fall of Norway in June 1940.

The Matador had optional four-wheel drive, with fully-floating axles with banjo housings. Brakes were originally air-pressure-assisted Lockheed hydraulics, but later full air-brakes were employed and the latter were always used on the RAF Matadors. The Army tractors, for medium artillery or heavy anti-aircraft guns, carried a crew of ten in the front part of the body, with space behind them for ammunition.

The most common body used by the RAF on its Matadors was a platform type often used for carrying heavy equipment or for towing a 20-ton 16-wheel Multiwheeler trailer. After the war the RAF also used the Matador as a signals van and as a power generator.

As well as for tractor work, the Army used some Matadors as portees for carrying 25 pounder guns, while an armoured version called the Deacon was used as a self-propelled 6 pounder anti-tank gun. Another armoured version was the Dorchester wireless control office used for communications between main and rear divisions in the North African campaign. Production of Dorchesters was 416 and of Deacons 175. Total production of Matadors between 1939 and 1945 was 9,029. They remained in service for many years after the war, being replaced eventually by AEC Militant and Leyland Martian tractors.

Their pulling power was legendary; on one occasion a Matador tow-started a Sherman tank on a rough, steep slope whilst on another occasion a Matador which was already towing a 4x4 3-ton truck and carrying a Jeep came across a 6x6 refuelling truck which had burnt out its clutch towing another 6x6 truck. The Matador simply added the two 6x6s to its 'train' and towed all three to the top of the Bulli Pass in Australia, and for 50 miles on into Sydney. Because of their towing ability, ex-Army Matadors were very popular with garages in the post-war years. Some were rebodied with later style AEC cabs, and a few can still be seen in service today.

The Scammell Pioneer (see page 49) was also used as a heavy artillery tractor, as was the Albion CX 22S, and in addition there were some interesting experimental designs. Among these was the Dennis Octolat, originally planned as an 8x8 from which it derived its name (Octo Light Artillery Tractor). It was never built with eight wheels, but the name was kept for the 6x6 prototypes, powered by two Bedford six-cylinder engines which drove the three axles via standard Bedford clutches and gearboxes, and a Dennis-made transfer box. The

Octolat had skid steering, like a tank, and the only springing was provided by its 10.00x20 Michelin Trak Grip tyres which weighed about 340 pounds each. The drive from two engines proved too complex however and they were replaced by a single 9.8-litre Leyland unit. This later version also had light armour and a central driving position. Only the one prototype was ever made.

Another experimental artillery tractor, and a more practical machine than the Octolat, was the Bedford Traclat. This was very closely based on the German halftrack vehicles which had proved so successful in the Libyan campaign in towing the 88mm Flak *(Flieger abwehr kanone)* gun. (see page 107). Captured examples were sent to England for evaluation, and Vauxhall Motors were asked to design an improved version. One problem was that of the power unit, for the German halftracks had engines developing between 100 and 230bhp, whereas the standard Bedford engine was a 72bhp, and they had nothing else until the 350bhp tank engine was available. The solution was to use two six-cylinder engines side-by-side under a wide bonnet, driving through separate propeller shafts to a team of transfer gears at the back of the gearbox. The combined power of both engines then passed through a single clutch to a five-speed gearbox. At the front of this gearbox was the Cletrac-type differential-control steering system, which transmitted drive to the track sprockets. For normal steering on roads the front wheels were used, but when the

Above: **Two Albion artillery tractors. Top is a CX22S 6x4, powered by a 9.1-litre six-cylinder engine, of which more than 500 were made between 1943 and 1945. Bottom is a low-profile tractor, the FT15N; this was a smaller vehicle with a 4.6-litre engine and weighing 13,215 pounds, as against the 23,380 of the CX22S. The FT15N had six-wheel drive and hydraulic brakes. Production did not start until January 1945 and continued until March 1946.**
(The Tank Museum, Bovington)

steering wheel was rotated through half its lock the controlled differential came into action, varying the speed of the tracks to give effective steering even in deep mud. The Traclat had a top speed of 30mph and a comfortable cruising speed of 25mph. It was intended for use as a field artillery tractor, or for the 17 pounder and Bofors anti-aircraft gun. Six prototypes were running by early 1945 and, had hostilities continued, the Bedford Traclat would almost certainly have been put into production. Trials were continued in Germany after the war, but with no immediate demand for such a vehicle it was never put into production.

Amphibians

At the outbreak of war none of the fighting powers had any amphibious vehicles in service, though the German Trippel four-seater car was in existence, and was soon to be put into production at the Bugatti factory at Molsheim. The American amphibious Jeep (Ford GPA) and DUKW were made in quantity from 1942 onwards, and the British Army used them in considerable numbers. However, it was felt that the demands of the Pacific war might cause the Americans to limit the number of DUKWs provided under 'lend-lease', so in 1942 the War Office asked the Thornycroft company to develop an amphibious load carrier with a payload of 4 tons, road speed of 40mph and water speed of

six mph, and the ability to climb a 1 in 6 gradient sandy or shingle beach.

Design began in December 1942, and within twelve weeks the prototype was ready for trials. The man in charge of the project, code-named Terrapin, was Charles Burton, one of the most talented engineers ever employed by Thornycroft. During 1931, he had been responsible for design of the unconventional Gilford front-wheel-drive double-decker bus. The trials of the Terrapin were very successful and the machine was put into production by Morris Commercial Cars Ltd, as Thornycroft's Basingstoke plant was fully occupied with other war projects. The Terrapin was powered by two Ford V8 engines, each one driving, by worm shaft, the four wheels on each side of the vehicle. The eight wheels were evenly spaced along the chassis, but the front pair, being raised above the ground in normal road use, were fitted with agricultural tractor-type 12.75x24 tyres. The original contract was for 500 Terrapins, which were made from June 1943 onwards. They gave valuable service during the Normandy landings, in Holland and the Rhine basin, but a shortcoming was that they were only suitable for operation in reasonably calm waters. There was not sufficient freeboard to prevent waves from breaking over the bows and eventually sinking the Terrapin.

In November 1944 a Terrapin Mark II appeared, designed with the Far East conflict in mind. It was of the same general layout as its predecessor, but was 7ft 8ins longer at 30ft 8ins, and was rated for a load of 5 tons. Its climbing capacity was a gradient of 1 in 3, and it could carry a winch, crane or 17 pounder gun. Tyre pressures could be varied from the driver's seat, according to the demands of the surface being covered. Because of the sudden ending of the Pacific War in August 1945, the Terrapin II was never needed and only prototypes were made. The only known surviving Terrapin is a Mark I which was used by the South of Scotland Electricity Board for ferrying personnel and equipment to the seawater intake towers of the Portobello Power Station, Edinburgh. It was still operational in the early 1970s.

The only other British-built amphibian of the period was a private venture called the Opperman Scorpion. Made by S.E Opperman Ltd of Borehamwood, Herts, who after the war made the unusual Motocart three-wheeled farm vehicle, the Scorpion was an 8x8, but the wheels were arranged in a highly unusual layout, with three axles in the centre of the vehicle and single wheels at the front and rear. The centre axle had a wider track than the other two and carried wheels of greater diameter. Powered by an outboard motor, the Scorpion was planned in two forms, an armoured fighting vehicle and a load carrier. However, only one prototype of the former was actually built.

Left: **A prototype of the Terrapin Mark II amphibian, rated for a 5 ton load and with cargo space of 310 cubic feet.**
(Transport Equipment Thornycroft Ltd)

CHAPTER TWO

British Commonwealth

Up to 1939 the Canadian Army relied largely
on commercial trucks of American design.

The transformation of the Canadian motor industry was one of the most remarkable stories of the war. Up to 1939 the Canadian Army relied largely on commercial trucks of American design which were built by subsidiaries of the 'Big Three', Ford, General Motors and Chrysler. No specifically military designs were available when war broke out in Europe, and when Canada declared war on Germany exactly a week after Great Britain. To meet British needs the Canadian Department of National Defence immediately stepped up production of civilian models which were known as Modified Conventional Vehicles. They received slight modifications to make them suitable for military work and comprised cars, utilities and trucks from $^3/_4$ ton to 3 tons capacity.

At the same time designs were drawn up for a new range of vehicles to meet British Army requirements. These used American-designed engines and running gear but were built to fit in with the standard British categories of 8cwt, 15cwt, 1 ton, 30cwt and 3 ton capacities. Four-wheel drive was envisaged for many of the models and they were to have standardised military-style cabs with semi-forward-control driving position. Contracts were placed with Ford Motor Company of Canada and General Motors of Canada, and a high degree of standardisation of parts was achieved. The main exception was that Ford-built vehicles used their familiar side-valve V8 engine while General Motors products used the Chevrolet

'stove-bolt six' engine. There was no time for prolonged testing of components and engineers were required almost overnight to make decisions which would normally have taken weeks or months. These decisions had to be backed with confidence so that the necessary materials could be ordered in large quantities, and if a component was found to be unsatisfactory when pilot models of trucks were built it had to be redesigned and retooled immediately. The result of this frantic activity was that although design did not begin until mid-September 1939, the first Canadian military trucks arrived in Britain with the Canadian forces in December. The standardised design was originally called the DND pattern (Department of National Defence), but when they came to be used by foreign armies the name CMP (Canadian Military Pattern) was chosen.

Despite the hurry with which they were put into production, few basic changes were made to the CMP design. One of the most important concerned the cab, which was found to be too cramped making the driving position very uncomfortable. This was modified in 1942 and the new cab also differed in having a forward sloping windscreen. This reduced glare and avoided the piling-up of snow and mud. There were several different cab designs, with the following designations:-

Type 11   original design of 1939-1941
Type 12   original design with alligator opening bonnet
Type 13   reverse slope windscreen 1942-1945

Type 41 as Type 11, but cowl only (India)
Type 42 as Type 12, but top removed
Type 43 as Type 13, but top removed
Type 43S extra wide with four seats

There were a number of small differences between CMPs made by Ford and by Chevrolet. These were as follows:-

	Chevrolet[1]	Ford
Engine, type	straight-six	V8
Axles (driven) type	banjo	split
Radiator grille mesh pattern	diagonal	square
Radiator grille badge type	Chevrolet	Ford (oval)
Radiator guard springs type	double leaf	laminated leaf
Radiator overflow tank position	exposed[2]	concealed
Horn position	concealed (on inlet manifold)	exposed (opposite steering box)
Steering wheel type (four spoke)	wood rim[3]	black hard rubber
Pre-1943 dash instruments[4]	GM commercial	Ford commercial

[1]Some 6x6 models used the large GMC 100bhp six-cylinder engine
[2]Concealed from 1943 (under left-hand floorboard)
[3]Pior to 1943 black hard rubber

[4]From 1943 universal circular instruments were used instead of the rectangular inherited from 1940-41 commercial trucks.

Production of all Canadian-built CMP types was 409,936, out of a total of 857,970 soft-skinned vehicles and over 50,000 armoured vehicles.

The following sections will deal largely with the CMP designs, as Canadian-built machines in the Modified Conventional Vehicle category were generally similar to those made in the United States, and to avoid repetition are described in that chapter.

8cwt, 4x2 and 4x4

The majority of CMP vehicles in the 8cwt class were 4x4s, but in the early years of the war a number were made with rear-wheel drive only. These included a Heavy Utility in the same class as the car-based Ford and Humber utilities and light trucks used for general duties and as wireless trucks. The Heavy Utilities, all made by Ford, were bodied in England by either Mulliner or Stewart & Ardern, and seated a crew of six including the driver. Most were used by the RAF. The trucks were known, logically, as C8 when made by Chevrolet and F8 when made by Ford.

In 1942 came the 4x4 version of the Heavy Utility and 8cwt truck, which was made in much greater numbers than the 4x2. They were known as the C8A and were built only by Chevrolet. The

Above: **A Chevrolet FAT (Field Artillery Tractor) also made by Ford, and was designated either the CGT or FGT. It has the earlier type cab and is towing a 25 pounder gun and limber.**
(The Tank Museum, Bovington)

Above far right and right: **The Chevrolet C60S was used as a breakdown tractor with Holmes swinging boom equipment. Each boom equipment had a separate winch driven from a power take off. Telescoping brace legs on each side relieved the frame when a side pull was in operation. These tractors were used for the recovery of lighter vehicles and guns.**
(The Tank Museum, Bovington)

Right: **A preserved Chevrolet C8a 4x4 with the later-type CMP cab. The heavy utility body could be used for a wide variety of duties; in this case a paymaster's vehicle and field office with the Royal Canadian Artillery Survey Regiment.**
(Nick Georgano)

drive to the front axle was made under patents from the Marmon-Herrington Co of Indianapolis who did a lot of conversion work on Chevrolet, Ford, Dodge and other chassis, as well as making heavy trucks of their own design. The C8A was built on the passenger-car assembly line at GM's Oshawa, Ontario, factory and was powered by the 3.5-litre 85bhp six-cylinder engine which was used in passenger cars from 1929 to 1953. Known as the 'Cast Iron Wonder' because of its cast iron pistons, this engine was used in all CMP trucks built by General Motors, except for some 6x6s which had the larger 4.4-litre GMC truck engine.

A wide variety of bodies was built on the C8A chassis. The most familiar was the six-passenger personnel carrier known as the Heavy Utility, Personnel, or HUP for short. It was used for transporting small parties or as a Commanding Officer's mobile office. The CO's evidently did not find it ideal for their purpose, and complained that it was 'very rough riding, noisy and finished in too spartan a manner'. Consequently a revised model known as the Staff Car went into production early in 1945. This had better sound-proofing by

mounting the transfer case in rubber and reducing gear noise by fitting an external contracting parking brake on the rear propeller shaft, this giving a flywheel effect. Ride comfort was improved by the use of larger and more flexible springs, while interior comfort was enhanced by insulation, linoleum on the floors, better lighting and a water heater.

Left: **Chevrolet 30 cwt trucks with Gotfredson ammunition-carrying welded bodies, used by the Long-Range Desert Group. This was a unit of the British Army formed in Egypt in 1940 to operate behind enemy lines. A patrol is about to leave the oasis which is the desert HQ of the LRDG. The nearest truck has had most of its grille removed for improved cooling.** *(IWM)*

Below far left: **A Chevrolet 30cwt 4x4 GS truck with the early type (1940/41) CMP cab, and 10ft all-steel body. It is one of the 1500 supplied to Britain in 1941.** *(NMM)*

Above: **This Ford-built CMP 3-ton truck is a F60S (F=Ford, 60cwt S=short wheelbase). The wheelbase was 134inches, compared with 158inches for the F60L.**
(Peter Daniels/NMM)

This staff car was officially intended for the use of a Commander and Adjutant, but not many were made before the war ended.

By contrast, more than 1000 HUPs were made, and many were purchased by UNRRA (United Nations Relief and Rehabilitation Administration) for use in Poland, Czechoslovakia and Yugoslavia. A total of 4,000 Canadian Army trucks were bought by UNRRA and many other were sold to the Dutch government for military or civilian use.

Other versions of the C8A included a wireless van (HUW – Heavy Utility, Wireless), ambulance (HUA – Heavy Utility, Ambulance), office or computer van (Heavy Utility, Computer; the abbreviation HUC was not used,) and 8cwt truck, which

Right: **Ford F60L with early type cab (1941) and British-built 3-ton GS body.**
(The Tank Museum, Bovington)

was supplied as a chassis/cab in CKD form. Few of these trucks were made and most of them seem to have gone to the Royal New Zealand Air Force. Some armoured personnel carriers were also built on the C8A chassis.

15 & 30cwt, 4x2, 4x4

These types were made by both Ford and Chevrolet and were used by British, South African, Australian and Indian troops as well as by Canadian. The 4x2s included trucks, open personnel carriers and platforms to carry a 20mm AA gun. The 15cwt models had the same 101¼in wheelbase as the 8cwts, but the 30cwts were on a 134in wheelbase. The Chevrolets used the 3.5-litre 'Cast Iron Wonder' engine and the Fords the 3.9-litre V8 as used in Mercury cars rather than the 'regular Ford' 3.6-litre V8. Depending on the manufacturer, the 30cwt models were known as C30 or F30. Body variants included office, ambulance, wireless and gun tractor. In the interests of standardisation the 30cwt models were dropped in 1943, being replaced by the 3 ton truck.

3 ton, 4x2, 4x4

A small number of 4x2s with CMP cabs were made by Ford, but the great majority of CMP trucks in this class were 4x4s. Indeed a high proportion of the 345,831 four-wheel-drive trucks made in Canada were in the 3 ton class. They were made in three wheelbases, 115in for tractors, 134in for short trucks and 158in for long trucks. Thus an F60L would be a long wheelbase Ford and a C60S a short wheelbase Chevrolet truck. There were many body variants, including ambulance, petrol or water tanker, cipher office (for coding and decoding messages), senior officers' caravan, signals van, dental clinic, disinfecter truck, instrument and machinery repair van, breakdown truck, kitchen and power auger for boring holes. There was also an Australian assembled Ford F60S or F60L with open cab and equipped with a 40mm AA gun. An

Above: **A Chevrolet 15cwt 4x4 GS truck passes through the German town of Gemen, 30 March 1945. Behind it is a Ford WOA2A heavy utility.** *(IWM)*

*Below:*Ford-built 3-tonners at the Rippleway Assembly Depot, Barking, Essex, in 1943. The trucks are F60Ls with composite wood and steel bodies. Large numbers of Chevrolet and Ford CMP trucks were assembled in Britain from CKD components, also in Egypt, Russia and China. In 1945/46 some were assembled for civilian use in Holland and Italy.
(Ford of Britain)

unusual model used in North Africa in 1942 was a Ford F60L with canvas tilt making it look like an ordinary truck, but concealing a 75mm gun under the canvas. These had armoured front ends.

3 ton, 6x4, 6x6

These were derived from the four-wheeled 3-ton trucks. The Ford F60H 6x4s had an unusual drive layout as they were derived from the 4x4 chassis. The front and leading rear axles were powered, and the rearmost axle was trailing, as opposed to the normal arrangement in which the rear axles are both driven and the front one unpowered. This was the system favoured by General Motors for the Chevrolet C60X. Most of the bodies on these chassis were van types for use as workshops, switchboards and X-ray units. Other uses included breakdown trucks, aircraft refuellers and bridging equipment carriers.

An experimental 6x6 3-ton truck was powered

by a 5.3-litre straight-eight Chrysler engine mounted in a GM chassis. Only five of these were made, with GS bodies which could be split for loading in a Dakota aircraft.

Artillery Tractors, 4x4

Ford and General Motors made 22,891 artillery tractors of CMP pattern between 1940 and 1945. They were built on the 101¼in C8A chassis and were known as the CGT or FGT according to the manufacturer, although the Canadian Army classified them as FATs (Field Artillery Tractor). They seated a crew of six including the driver and were used mainly for towing a 17 pounder anti-tank gun. Six successive body types were used; the first two types had two doors and a typical artillery tractor body similar to those on the Guy Quad Ant or Morris Commercial C8. Later bodies were less specialised and used the standard CMP cab. The third, fourth and fifth types had four doors, the fifth being

Left: **The gun tractor on the 101in wheelbase was known to the Army as an FAT (Field Artillery Tractor), but in the makers' own terminology it was a CGT or FGT (Chevrolet or Ford Gun Tractor). This is an early type (pre-1942) CGT with the sloping roof cab of the Morris-Commercial Quads.**
(NMM)

Left: **This dramatic photograph shows an early type CGT with a canvas cover obscuring the two-tier windscreen struggling through a flooded river near Cesena, south of Ravenna, in October 1944. A Chevrolet 30cwt waits on the bank.**
(IWM)

Below far left: **Ford F60H with early-type cab and open body. Most six-wheeled CMP trucks had van bodies for a wide variety of specialist uses, mobile workshops, laboratories, X-ray vans and switchboards.**
(The Tank Museum, Bovington)

Above: **Six-wheeled trucks of CMP pattern were made with either 6x4 or 6x6 wheel-drive. This is a Chevrolet C60X 6x6 van used by the Royal Canadian Electrical & Mechanical Engineers as a mobile testing station for equipment such as starters and generators. Behind the driver's door are two small doors covering the ventilator for the generator engine.**
(Public Archives of Canada)

Above right: **A later type Ford FGT with reverse-slope windscreen and flatter cab top. An identical looking model was also made by Chevrolet.**
(Ford of Britain)

winterised for operations in temperatures as low as -20°F. The final Canadian-built model had a tarpaulin-topped open body closer in appearance to the ordinary C8A truck. There were also some Australian-built models with their own characteristics.

In addition to the short-wheelbase tractors, some 4x4 3 ton units on the 134in wheelbase were used for pulling artillery. In these the open GS body had ammunition lockers in the forward part and accommodation for seven crew behind. Equipment included a winch driven from the power take-off, a tow hook and storage for a spare gun barrel.

AUSTRALIA & NEW ZEALAND

No specifically military vehicles were made in Australia before the war, and the bulk of their fleet consisted of Canadian chassis with locally made bodywork, together with a few chassis of British origin, mostly Bedfords. In 1940, the first CMP trucks were assembled in Australia, and these soon became a major product of the Australian Ford and General Motors plants, although they also made a

variety of trucks, pickups and ambulances of American design. The CMP cabs were known in Australia as CWO (Canadian War Office), although they generally went by the nickname 'Blitz'.

General Motors-Holden Pty Ltd, who today make the well known Holden cars, concentrated production of 'Blitz' cabs at their Woodville, South Australia factory, with chassis and other types of vehicle being made at Pagewood, New South Wales, or Fisherman's Bend, Victoria. Ford had assembly plants at Sydney, Brisbane, Adelaide and Fremantle.

Australian 'Blitz' models were similar to the Canadian ones except for minor details of the cab design, but there were some specifically Australian versions. These included van-type, artillery tractors on the Chevrolet CGT chassis. Australia also made other local designs, such as coupé utilities (the popular 'Utes' beloved of outback farmers) on Ford, Chevrolet and Dodge chassis and some experimental halftrack conversions on Ford, Chevrolet and International chassis. Holdens built a total of 14,248 bodies on 'Blitz' chassis and 9,847 on other chassis, while total Ford wartime production was 35,146 trucks, as well as 4x4 and 6x6 armoured vehicles.

Only Ford operated a plant in New Zealand, at Lower Hutt, which turned out 1,162 'Blitz' types, 3,611 modified conventional vehicles and 427 other types including staff cars.

INDIA

The only plant making military vehicles was Ford Motor Co of India Ltd, a subsidiary of the Canadian company. They assembled various CMP and other designs for which they manufactured the bodywork. An exception to this was the rear-engined Ford wheeled armoured carrier, for which bodywork was manufactured by the East Indian Railway Workshops and the Tata Iron & Steel Company. The latter assembled Mercedes-Benz trucks after the war, and today make all-Indian trucks and buses which still bear some resemblance to Mercedes-Benz designs. A total of 4,655 armoured carriers were made. In all, Ford of India made 64,216 4x2 vehicles 45,213 4x4s and 11,614 civilian type cars and trucks.

SOUTH AFRICA

Ford and General Motors both had South African assembly plants at Port Elizabeth. The Ford plant assembled a number of different American types, and also manufactured bodywork and front-wheel drive conversions of Marmon-Harrington design. Total Ford production at Port Elizabeth was 34,869.

Left: **Tractor/Trailer versions of the CMP range were known as F60T. The tractor was on a 115-inch wheelbase, and the trailers were non-detachable. They were rated for a 6 ton payload. Photographed in February 1945 this column is about to move out from the Porte de Versailles, Paris, to collect food supplies from a depot outside the city. The trucks were operated by French Army Transport Regiment.**
(IWM)

Left: **A Ford F60B with 40mm Bofors AA gun on a reinforced chassis with an extra wide cab seating a crew of four. Though mainly for anti-aircraft work, the gun would be effectively used against ground targets. Projecting from the rear is a spare barrel.**
(Dr. William A Gregg)

CHAPTER THREE

Germany

Once the Nazi party had come to power an enormous boost was
given to the development of military vehicles.

n complete contrast to Britain, Germany invested vast sums of money in developing military vehicles, in a series of programmes which began several years before Hitler's coming to power in January 1933. Between 1927 and 1929 a programme was laid down stressing the importance of cross-country mobility in the next generation of army vehicles, particularly those used for carrying troops. Figures were stipulated governing freedom of movement between the driving axles, ground clearance, front and rear overhang, centre of gravity and wading ability. At first there was little finance available, but several manufacturers produced pilot designs for six-wheeled staff cars. These included 6x4s from Horch and Mercedes-Benz and a 6x6 from Selve of Hamelin. The Mercedes-Benz G1 of 1926/8 was particularly significant as it was the ancestor of a line of six-wheeled staff cars made up to 1939 and favoured by Hitler and other party leaders as parade cars.

In November 1931, four German vehicle makers, Audi, DKW, Horch and Wanderer, combined to form Auto Union AG. This new group had government backing as a source of military machinery, as well as building a team of revolutionary racing cars which, with Mercedes-Benz, dominated Grand Prix racing from 1934 to 1939. Once the Nazi party had come to power an enormous boost was given to the development of military vehicles; in a publication of 1934 entitled *Wehrgeistige Erziehung* (Instructions for Military Planning), Lt. Col. Nehring stressed that the motor industry

should be financially supported by all the army commands in order to make sure that due regard to military interest was observed in actual construction. In other words, the motor industry was to be thought of primarily as a supplier of military needs, rather than a commercial organisation which might, or might not, provide a few vehicles for the army from time to time, as was the case in most other Western countries.

Exact figures for government investment in the motor industry will probably never be available, but Winston Churchill ascertained that German military spending as a whole rose from 5 million marks in 1933 to 8 million in 1934 and to 11 million in 1935, and this proportion was probably roughly maintained with regard to motor industry expenditure. Nehring also said that the motor factories were to be kept free from international ties and protected from foreign influence. This was particularly important for the German branches of multinational companies, Ford (Taunus) and General Motors (Opel), whose management in Detroit might not look with favour on a predominantly military programme. By 1937 German Fords, both cars and trucks, used 100% German materials.

In the mid 1930s, 36 German companies were making military or potentially military vehicles (including motorcycles). In order to reduce the multiplicity of types, the government laid down specifications for a series of Einheits (Standard) vehicles in six categories, light, medium and heavy personnel carriers and light, medium and heavy

load carriers. All these vehicles were to have four-wheel drive and some of them four-wheel steering. Engines were not standardised and so could be of the manufacturers' existing designs, so long as they were generally suitable in size, power output and governed speed. Some very advanced designs were built in the various Einheitstyp categories, but in 1938 a new plan was formulated by General Major von Schell, commander in chief of the Army Korps K. This called for a great reduction in the number of vehicle types made, not only military but civilian vehicles as well, and the effects of the Schell plan were felt beyond the German frontiers. As a result of Hitler's aid to General Franco in the Spanish Civil War, Spain came under German economic influence and the German plan for Europe did not envisage an industrialised Spain, where development of cars was discouraged. This led to the abandonment of at least one promising light car design, the Nacional-G.

Under the Schell Plan, the number of truck types made in Germany (which now included Austria and Czechoslovakia) was to be reduced from 113 to 19, of cars from 55 to 30 and of motorcycles from 150 to 30. The Leichter Einheits Pkw (light standard car) which had been made by BMW, Hanomag and Stoewer, was to be replaced by one car model, the Volkswagen Kübelwagen, and there were similar rationalisations in the heavier classes. Schell was horrified to discover that in 1938 the German ancillary industry was turning out 112 different types of brake cylinder, 113 starters, 164

dynamos and 264 lamp bulbs. All this was to be swept away, and he ordered that, for example, all 3-ton trucks should use only one kind of direction indicator, tail light, instrument panel, dynamo, etc.

Despite the ideals of standardisation, when the German Army went to war they used a great variety of vehicles, because many impressed civilian types were needed to make up numbers. The Dutch military vehicle historian Bart Vanderveen recalls that, in his home town of Assen, the civilian vehicles used by the occupying German forces outnumbered the real military types by something like a hundred to one. The variety of machinery was greatly increased by the British and American models captured after the evacuation of Dunkirk and by vehicles made for the Germans by French, Czech and Italian manufacturers. The result was the opposite of what General Schell had planned and, as the war progressed, more and more vehicles became inoperable because of the shortage of some simple component.

Of the types envisaged under the Schell plan, only the Volkswagen Kübel and the Mercedes-Benz and Steyr heavy personnel carriers and 1½-ton trucks ever went into mass production.

Staff Cars and Personnel Carriers

Before the introduction of the Einheits programme in 1934, a wide variety of makes were used as military cars and many of them survived in Army service up to the war years.

Above: **The standardised Einheits-Lkw 6x6 2½-ton truck was developed by MAN and made by them and five other manufacturers, Borgward, Büssing-NAG, Faun, Henschel and Magirus. This one, with standard truck body, is crossing an improvised bridge. In the foreground is a Renault AGK1 6-ton truck, either captured from the French army or made at Billancourt for the Wehrmacht.**
(The Tank Museum, Bovington)

Right: **Typical of a civilian-type staff car used by German officers is this Adler Diplomat 3-litre tourer.**
(IWM)

Below: **An early 1930s Kübelwagen on the Mercedes-Benz 260 chassis, with body by Gaubschat. Later versions had doors.**
(Daimler-Benz)

Left: A Mercedes-Benz G5 demonstrates its four-wheel steering. More than 300 of these were made between 1937 and 1941, some with half doors and some with full doors. A number were used by the Hungarian Army after the war. (Daimler-Benz)

The characteristic body style was the so called Kübelsitzer or 'bucket seat' which consisted of steel tube, folding seats in a doorless body made of plywood with a simple canvas hood. After 1937 doors were generally provided. There were four main types: the light car with two seats and a boot, the light car with four seats and the medium car with four seats, with or without boot. The vehicles with boots were used as telephone, radio or weapons carriers, while the others were purely passenger vehicles. Unlike the larger Einheits models, they were not intended as troop carriers but for the use of staff officers. Kübelsitzers could also be used as tractors for light guns.

Before the Reichswehr was transformed by the Nazi regime into the Wehrmacht, there was no central purchasing organisation - individual army commands were responsible for securing their transport, which explains the wide variety of chassis on which the Kübelsitzers were built. Among these were the Adler Favorit, BMW Dixi (German-built Austin Seven), BMW 303, DKW Meisterklasse, Hanomag Garant, Horch 830, various models · of Mercedes-Benz, including

Left: A Kübelwagen on the 3-litre Adler chassis, known as the 3Gd. Like other Kübelwagens it was designed to carry four soldiers and their kit, and to tow light artillery. In army terms it was classified Kfz.12, while the similar car without towing bracket was the Kfz.11. (Bart Vanderveen Collection)

Right: **The Leichter Einheits Geländegängige Personen- kraftwagen as made by Stoewer from 1936 to 1943. It used Stoewer's own 2-litre ohv four-cylinder engine, four- wheel drive and optional four- wheel steering. The Kfz.1 was a four-seater personnel carrier, Kfz.2 a signals car, Kfz.3 a light surveying car, and Kfz.4 carried an anti-aircraft gun.** *(School of Tank Technology)*

Types 170, 200, 290 and 320. In addition there were numerous models of impressed Axis cars and captured cars of all kinds.

The next stage in the development of personnel carriers came with the Einheits programme of 1934 onwards. Realising that the ordinary passenger car chassis could not be developed further, the Heereswaffenamt (Army Ordnance Office) laid down specifications for a new purpose-built series of vehicles with particular stress on cross-country mobility, of which the passenger vehicles were to be made in three categories, Leichter, Mittelschwerer and Schwerer Enheits Geländegängiger Personenkraftwagen (Light, Medium and Heavy Standard Cross-Country Passenger Car). The light version had an engine made by either BMW (1991cc 45bhp six-cylinder), Hanomag (1991cc 50bhp four-cylinder) or Stoewer (1750cc 43bhp or 1997cc 50bhp, both four-cylinder). Transmission was by a standardised five-speed gearbox to all four wheels. Bottom gear was 8.83:1 which enabled the cars to be driven at the speed of marching infantry-men, while direct-drive top gave a speed of 50mph. Four-wheel steering could be optionally engaged whilst the car was moving. Laden weight with the standard four-seater body was 2000kg. All wheels were sprung independently by coil springs, with double-action hydraulic shock absorbers.

The first of the Leichter Einheits models was made by Stoewer in 1936 and five different variants were made up to 1943, including radio vehicles and cars equipped with anti-aircraft guns. BMW built 3,225 between 1937 and 1940 and the Hanomag was made during the same period. In 1940 a simplified model appeared, called the Type 40. This

Left and Below:
Mercedes-Benz contribution to the light cross-country vehicle programme was the G5, powered by the company's 2-litre side-valve engine. It was less powerful than the ohv Stoewer of the same size. It was not ordered by the Wehrmacht in large numbers; only 300 were made between 1937 and 1941. Some were used by the Hungarian Army after the war. *(NMM)*

had front-wheel steering only and was made by Stoewer, BMW and Hanomag with a 2-litre Stoewer AW2 engine.

The Mittleschwerer Einheits cars were generally similar to the light models apart from having more powerful engines and front-wheel steering only. They also had an auxiliary gearbox which, with a four-speed main gearbox, gave a total of eight forward speeds. Most of the medium cars used a Horch V8 engine of either 3.5 or 3.8 litres, but some were made by Opel with that company's 3.6-litre six-cylinder Admiral engine. A greater variety of bodies was provided on the medium chassis: the basic style was a four-passenger open car, but there were also closed cars and vans used for radio communications, surveying, telephone exchange, cable testing and propaganda work. The propaganda vehicles were particularly used on the Russian front, broadcasting messages about the invincible might of the Wehrmacht both to soldiers and to the civilian population.

A characteristic of all the medium cars in the Einheits programme was that the spare wheels were carried at the side of the body, originally outside it, and from 1940 onwards inside the hull which allowed for a considerably wider body. Like the other Einheits models, the medium cars were much more sophisticated than anything that was available to Allied troops. Writing in *The Autocar* about a captured example in 1943, their correspondent said "although the vehicle is very unlovely, it is a sheer joy to drive: the suspension, steering and weight distribution being just right and long runs at high speed being quite effortless."

Daimler Benz did not receive any contracts under the Einheits Program, but in 1936 they produced a car in the same class as the Mittleschwerer with 2-litre engine and optional four-wheel steering. Forty-two of the first series, with open bodies and canvas doors, were supplied in 1936. These were known as the 170VL/W139 and the makers were encouraged to make a further 320 between 1937 and 1941. Known as the G5/W152, these versions had canvas or steel doors and could be had with fully convertible bodywork. Few of this series were bought by the Army and many of them went to mountain rescue services.

The Schwerer Einheits cars differed considerably from their smaller sisters in that their Horch V8 engines were rear-mounted. This layout was chosen so that the chassis could be adapted easily to fit an armoured car body, but it also provided plenty of body space behind a short, wide bonnet. The first model was made by Auto Union from 1935 to 1940 when it was superseded by an improved version with engine enlarged from 3.5 to 3.8 litres and hydraulic in place of mechanical brakes. A front-engined model was also made and both versions were built by Ford as well as Auto Union, these having the standard 3.6-litre Ford V8 engine. Four-wheel steering was optional but the simplified versions made from 1940 onwards employed only front-wheel steering. Like the smaller Einheits series, these were called the Model 40. As well as

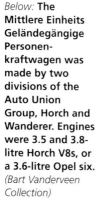

Below: **The Mittlere Einheits Geländegängige Personen-kraftwagen was made by two divisions of the Auto Union Group, Horch and Wanderer. Engines were 3.5 and 3.8-litre Horch V8s, or a 3.6-litre Opel six.** *(Bart Vanderveen Collection)*

Above: **A Tatra Type 57K Kübelwagen made in 1942 and in the insignia of the 10th Panzer Division, 'Frundsberg'.**
(Vehicle displayed at the Victory Memorial Museum)

Left: **Volkswagen's offering in the Kübelwagen field used the running gear of the familiar Beetle saloon. This one is in the insignia of the 21st Panzer Division, Afrika Corps. It has 690x 200 oversize tyres for desert use.**
(Vehicle displayed at the Victory Memorial Museum)

Right: **A Stoewer Leichter Einheits gl.pkw (Light Einheits-type cross-country passenger car) with four-wheel drive and optional four-wheel steering. This Type 3 light surveying car is in the insignia of the 11th Panzer Division.**
(Vehicle displayed at the Victory Memorial Museum)

Below: **A Steyr 1500 A/02 4x4 with crew cab used as a fire engine by the 79th Infantry Division.**
(Vehicle displayed at the Victory Memorial Museum)

Left: **A VW Schwimmwagen which carried Porsche type number 166 and the military designation K2s.** *(Vehicle displayed at the Victory Memorial Museum)*

Below: **One of several types of halftrack truck was this Opel 2 tonner. It used the standard 3.5-litre six-cylinder engine driving the front sprockets through a five-speed gearbox.** *(Vehicle displayed at the Victory Memorial Museum)*

Right: **Two Opels, left, a standard 3.5-ton general purpose truck, unusual in having a bus-type cab built by Friedrich Rometsch of Berlin. This company became well-known after the war for cabriolet bodies on Volkswagens. On the right is a smaller Opel, a 1-ton light truck which served as an ambulance with an anti-tank unit.** *(Vehicles displayed at the Victory Memorial Museum)*

Left: **The Krupp L2H143 Protze or 'Schnautzer' was an unusual-looking but practical light 6x4 powered by an air-cooled flat-four engine. As well the GS truck shown here, it was used as a gun tractor, searchlight truck, personnel carrier and radio van. There was also an armoured version.**
(J Spencer-Smith)

Below: **A Phänomen Granit Type 25H of the 3rd Panzer Division. These air-cooled vehicles were among the most popular ambulances in use by the Wehrmacht.**
(Vehicle displayed at the Victory Memorial Museum)

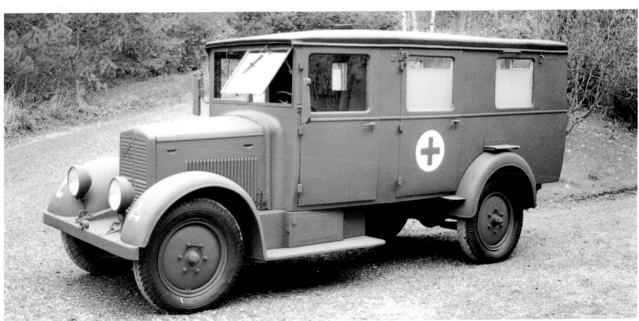

Right: **A Mercedes-Benz ambulance Type L1500S which served with the 12th SS Panzer Division, Hitlerjugend.** *(Vehicle displayed at the Victory Memorial Museum)*

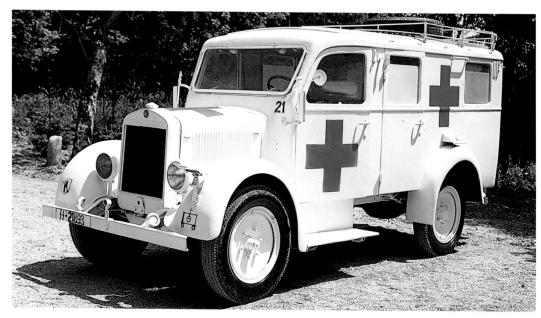

Centre: **A light halftrack Kfz 11 powered by a 100bhp six-cylinder Maybach engine. This one was built by Borgward, but the same design was also made by Adler, Auto Union, Hanomag and Skoda.** *(Vehicle displayed at the Victory Memorial Museum)*

Below: **Two examples of the unusual Kettenkrad which combined a halftrack with the front forks of a motorcycle. The 1.5-litre 36bhp Opel Olympia engine gave it a top speed of 50mph (80km/h).** *(Vehicle displayed at the Victory Memorial Museum)*

Above: **One of the later type of Raupenschlepper-Ost (tracked tractor, east) with open cab, wooden doors and body and Deutz diesel engine. A Steyr design, this example was built by Klockner-Humboldt-Deutz.** *(Vehicle displayed at the Victory Memorial Museum)*

Left: **A Hanomag-built example of the Kfz 11 light halftrack. It could seat 14 passengers and had a towing capacity of 3 tons. This vehicle is extremely rare.** *(Vehicle displayed at the Victory Memorial Museum)*

Above: **The lightest of the German halftracks was the Sd.Kfz 10 for towing a 1 ton load. Designed and developed by Demag as the D7, it was also made by Adler, Büssing-NAG, MIAG, Phänomen and Saurer.**
(Vehicle displayed at the Victory Memorial Museum)

Right: **A late model halftrack in the Sd.Kfz 11 class was this Auto-Union-built version of 1944. It has the Einheits-type cab and wooden body for a 2 1/2 ton load.**
(Vehicle displayed at the Victory Memorial Museum)

Above: **This Horch m.gl. E. Pkw was among the first German vehicles to enter Tobruk in June 1942. Unusually, the spare wheel is carried inside the vehicle, not in an inset panel on the body side.**
(IWM)

Left: **This view of the Auto Union-built heavy cross-country car shows the spare wheel mounting in the body side. This is a Type 11 front-engined car, the rear-engined Type 1 chassis being reserved for armoured body-work.**
(School of Tank Technology)

commercial cars, the Schwerer models were used for radio and telephone communications, as ambulances, light artillery tractors, light air defence vehicles and searchlight vehicles, and for carrying motorised rifle regiments.

Before looking at the replacements for the Einheits Program, it is worth considering a few vehicles which were contemporary with the standard cars, though of completely different design. The Austrian Steyr company, famous for armaments and a car manufacturer since 1920, built 1,200 of their Type 250, a Kübelwagen on their light truck chassis. These were made from 1938 to 1940 but were not so satisfactory for cross-country work as their German contemporaries since they had only two-wheel drive. Steyr later made a very

successful 4x4 command car, but as this was a replacement for the Einheits series, it is covered in a later section.

In Czechoslovakia the Tatra company had been making unconventional air-cooled cars since 1923 and from 1938 onwards supplied the Wehrmacht with a number of Kübelwagen based on their Type 57 passenger car. They also made a streamlined saloon with rear-mounted 3-litre V8 engine, some of which were 'acquired' by German officers in Czechoslovakia. Their handling was unpredictable because of the concentration of weight at the rear, and after a number of fatal accidents the German High Command began to suspect that they were a Czech secret weapon, and forbade them to all personnel. A different Tatra was the V809, a 4x4 open

four-seater in the medium-car class, powered by a 2470cc four-cylinder air-cooled engine. A number of these were used by Field Marshal Rommel's Afrika Korps, their air-cooling being very welcome in the blistering desert heat. One was fitted with a saloon body and 4-litre V8 engine for the personal use of Rommel himself.

The six-wheeled command car was a peculiarly German vehicle, though some had been made in the early 1930s by Morris Commercial. The best known was the Mercedes-Benz G4, powered by the 5-litre straight-eight engine used in the Type 500K passenger car. It was developed from the six-cylinder G1 six-wheeler of 1926 to 1928 and was intended for cross-country military use. However, it proved to be too heavy at 3500kg for this work, as

well as extremely expensive, and of the 57 made during 1933/34, most were used as open parade cars by Hitler, Goering and other leaders. The G4 was especially favoured by Hitler, and was used by him for really important occasions, such as his entry into Czechoslovakia at Wildenau in October 1938, and his tour of Prague in March 1939. One G4 chassis was fitted with a communications van body and used in Hitler's fleet for the convenience of press reporters. In 1939 a few G4s had their 5-litre engines replaced by the 5.4-litre unit of the Type 540K car, but it is not thought that any complete G4s were built after 1934. Of the 57 made only one is thought to survive today.

Other six-wheelers were made by Krupp, Steyr, Praga, Skoda and Tatra. The nearest to a passenger

Above: **Holsters for Luger pistols fitted to interior door panels.**
(Daimler-Benz)

car design that Krupp, the famous armaments firm, ever came was their L2H149. It had a 52bhp 3.3-litre four-cylinder engine, and was in effect a passenger version of a light truck chassis. The body was a fully convertible six-seater and the overall weight about 3000kg. Although 500kg lighter than the Mercedes-Benz G4 it had little more than half the power, so cannot have been a very lively performer. Only a handful were made from 1939–40.

The Steyr 640 was a development of a 6x4 truck chassis, as was the Praga AV. This had a 3460cc six-cylinder engine and a three-speed gearbox with two-speed auxiliary, whereas the RV truck had a four-speed main gearbox. The AV had a substantial body consisting of a six-seater convertible with a luggage locker behind, long and wide enough to carry two horizontally mounted spare wheels side-

by-side. A total of 389 Praga AVs were made from 1936 to 1939, initially for the Czech Army, but also, after 1938, for the Wehrmacht. Skoda also made 6x4 commercial cars powered by the 3140cc Superb engine, initially for their own home use and from 1941 to 1943 for the Germans. The same situation applied to the Tatra T82 and T93, the latter a 6x6 truck-based design.

As we have seen, the Schell Plan effectively killed off the Einheits models, and the bold dreams of 1934 with a fleet of all independently sprung, four-wheel-drive and steering vehicles gave way to much more conventional machines from 1940 onwards. Not that the Einheits models were phased out of use - the Wehrmacht was much too short of transport for that – but they were too complex to make and particularly to service in the field.

Left: **Earlier models did not have the step for access to the rear seats. The car Hitler used during the war had handgrips at the side of the windscreen pillars, by which he pulled himself into the front seat. The G4 could be equipped with machine guns; all had open tourer bodies except for two radio communications vans and one luggage van.**
(Daimler-Benz)

Simplicity and robustness were the prime criteria once the Wehrmacht was engaged in war.

The light cars of the Einheits Program were replaced in 1940 by the Mercedes-Benz 170V, and from 1941 by the Volkswagen Kübelwagen. The Mercedes was based on the firm's popular pre-war passenger car, having a 38bhp 1.7-litre four-cylinder engine. Two body styles were seen on the military version, the Kfz 2/40 with three seats and a boot, and the Kfz 3 with four seats and a boot. They were used as communications, radio or light repair vehicles. In production from 1938 to 1942, a total of 19,000 170Vs were made for the Wehrmacht.

On 1 November 1941, General von Schell reported to Hitler that all the existing light and medium personnel carriers were to be replaced by a single model, the Type 82 Kübelwagen made by Volkswagen. The first Volkswagen saloon cars had been made in 1935 and by 1938 two pre-production series of 30 cars each had been built and tested. The open military version was designed in 1936 and was ready for testing in 1939. It had the same 998cc air-cooled flat-flour engine as the saloon, and the same platform chassis with its central tube, bifurcated at the rear to support the engine and transmission. All four wheels were independently sprung by torsion bars. The body was a simple open four-seater made of 18-gauge steel pressings. Unlike the earlier Kübelsitzer it had four proper doors and the spare wheel was carried on the bonnet, inset on the early models but mounted above the bonnet on production versions from 1940 onwards. This made for a less costly bonnet pressing and also enabled the wheel to be detached more

easily. The bodies were to have been made at the new Volkswagen plant at Wolfsburg, but as the body shops were not completed in time they were made by Ambi-Budd in Berlin and sent to Wolfsburg.

The first prototypes were ready shortly before the invasion of Poland on 1 September 1939, and were used in that campaign. They were not well received at first, being criticised for their lack of four-wheel drive and their low ground clearance. The former could not be remedied quickly, although a 4x4 version was made later, but the ground clearance was improved, door sills raised and many other details changed on the production models which were made from February 1940 onwards. Strictly speaking, the prototypes were designated Porsche Type 62, as they came from the Porsche design bureau, and the production models, Volkswagen Type 82.

After some development the air-cooled engine proved very reliable and on the whole the Kübelwagens were well received. In the desert they were found to be greatly superior to motorcycles, which they replaced, and could negotiate any surface except shifting sand dunes. Some components gave trouble, in particular clutches, front and rear suspensions and wheel bearings. For desert work distributors and dynamos needed to be made dust-proof. From March 1943 onwards all models had a larger engine of 1131cc (also used in post-war VW cars), as a result of a decree from the Heereswaffenamt that no military vehicle should have engines of less than 25bhp.

The main uses of the Type 82 were as a four-seater personnel carrier, repairs car, surveying car, two-seater siren car, two-stretcher ambulance and three-seater radio vehicle. There were also a number of variants on the basic design including the Type 166 Schwimmwagen (see amphibians), the Type 157 modified to run on railway lines, the Type 155 halftrack Kübel, Type 235 electric-powered Kübel and Type 276 Kübel with towing hook. A large number were fitted with producer-gas engines (Type 230) and there were experimental models with five-speed gearboxes (Type 177 or 178) and fuel injection (Type 179). About 55,000 Type 82s were made, and 15,000 of all other models including the amphibians. Although large for Germany, these figures were dwarfed by the 639,245 Jeeps built between 1941 and 1945.

The Kübelwagen survived in civilian use for many years after the war, a number being used as postal vans in the immediate post-war years. So great was their appeal that in 1970 the makers brought out an updated open car on the Kübel theme, the 181 or 'The Thing' as it was nicknamed. This was made, latterly in Mexico, until 1982.

The heavy Einheits cars were probably the least successful of all the models, being too heavy and very costly to maintain. After 1942 they were replaced in production by an Austrian design, the Steyr 1500, built as personnel carrier, command car and light truck. It was a substantial machine weighing 3620kg and powered by a 3.5-litre air-cooled V8 engine developing 85bhp. It had independent

Left: **A VW Kübelwagen demonstrates its hill climbing ability.** *(Jonathon Wood Collection)*

Below: **A VW Kübelwagen with General Reichelt in the rear seat, under British supervision at the end of the war.** *(IWM)*

front suspension by torsion bars and optional four-wheel drive with two-speed auxiliary gearbox. The command car was a comfortable four-door convertible, used by General von Arnim and others, while the personnel carrier was a full eight-seater. These Steyr 1500s were made not only in Austria, but in Germany by Auto Union. A total of 18,850 were made by Steyr and several thousand more by Auto Union. The only other personnel carriers made in the new 1500 class were the Mercedes-Benz L1500S (4x2) and L1500A (4x4) and the Phänomen Granit 4x4 with 2.7-litre six-cylinder air-cooled engine. Its absence of water to boil or freeze made it popular both with the Afrika Korps and on the Russian Front.

Amphibians

Unlike Britain and the United States, Germany did not make any large amphibious trucks, but they made two types of light car, the equivalent of the amphibious Jeep. The first was the Trippel which had been made commercially in small numbers

since 1934, initially with a four-cylinder Adler engine and, from 1937, with a six-cylinder Opel Kapitan engine. In 1939 Hans Trippel was asked by the Heereswaffenamt to develop a military version of his four-cylinder car, and this went into service with the Todt labour organisation, and was later used by Army units. It had a land speed of 40mph and a water speed of 4½ knots.

More important was the Opel-powered SG6, of which about a thousand were made from 1940 to 1944. This was a full four-seater open car with front mounted engine, three-speed gearbox and four-wheel drive. The propeller was pivoted about the same axis as the driveshaft and could be raised or lowered by a lever to the left of the driver. Four-wheel steering was provided for driving on land, but in the water the Trippel could be steered only by the front wheels, which must have made for rather a slow response to the steering wheel.

From 1940 to 1942 Trippel cars were built in part of the Bugatti factory at Molsheim, where 350 were made. The balance came from Trippel's own factory at Homburg, Saar. Most were used by the Waffen SS, the military branch of the SS. Variants included a saloon version of the SG6 and an eight-seater carrying a 37mm gun and two 7.92mm machine guns.

The last Trippel design was the SG7 built in 1943. This was powered by a rear-mounted Tatra V8 engine and had a doorless body. It was the basis for an amphibious armoured car called the Schildkrote (Tortoise). After the war Trippel made a small car powered by a rear-mounted, flat-twin, Zündapp engine, and in 1961 returned to the amphibian theme with the Amphicar, of which 2500 were made up to 1968.

Left: **Ferdinand Porsche stands next to a Schwimmwagen contemplating another of his designs, the enormous Maus, the largest tank made during World War Two.** *(IWM)*

Below: **The Schwimmwagen's propeller was lowered manually to engage with a dog clutch attached to a power take-off from the engine.** *(Volkswagen)*

A much more important amphibious car was the VW Schwimmwagen, of which the first batch were made in 1940. It was to replace motorcycle combinations in motorised formations, hence its original name, Kradschützen Ersatzwagen (motorcycle troops replacement vehicle). Most mechanical components were similar to those in the Kübelwagen and the first series of 150 had the same wheelbase of 2400mm. This was reduced to 2000mm in 1941, when the finalised design appeared. Unlike the Kübelwagen, all Schwimmwagen had four-wheel drive, and they were very effective in cross-country work as well as in the water. Most of the 14,625 made were used on the Russian front for reconnaissance by SS tank units. For starting in cold weather an especially volatile fuel was employed, which was kept in a 1-litre tank in the engine compartment. The main fuel tanks, two of 25 litres each, were in the front. The spare wheel was also in front, while down the sides were kept a spade and two paddles. The latter helped with steering in cramped spots for, like the Trippel, the Schwimmwagen had no aids to steering apart from the front wheels. The first series were known as the Porsche 128 and the main batch as the VW166.

Trucks

The history of German military trucks, like that of cars and personnel carriers, falls into three eras, the pre-standardisation period when a wide variety of mostly civilian models were taken into military service, the Einheits models, and the final rationalisation under the Schell plan. As with the cars, trucks were divided into road-going and cross-country types.

During the 1920s the German Army was small and restricted in its activities and the trucks it acquired were all commercial models. The first moves towards specifically military trucks came in 1929 when the War Ministry laid down specifications for a 6x4 with a capacity of 1½ tons on roads and 1 ton across country. Three manufacturers responded to this, Büssing-NAG, Daimler Benz and Magirus, joined later by Henschel and Krupp.

The most popular Büssing-NAG was the G31, powered by a 3920cc 65bhp four-cylinder engine, of which 2300 were made between 1931 and 1935. Another model from this old established Brunswick manufacturer was the 3G16, powered by a 9350cc 90bhp engine, of which about 300 were made from 1931 to 1938, which could carry double the G31's load of 1500kg.

Daimler Benz began production with the 1500 and 1800kg G3 and G3a, later joined by the 3000kg Lg J3000 diesel of which 7434 were made between 1935 and 1938.

Left: **A Schwimmwagen in company with other Wehrmacht vehicles including a BMW R75 motorcycle with sidecar.** *(IWM)*

Right: **German-built Fords used similar sheet metal and V8 engines to their American counterparts though later examples had the Einheits cab and there were forward control variants not seen in America.**
(Ford of Germany)

Right: **The Opel Blitz was produced in large numbers from 1937 to 1944, and earned a good reputation in all fields of war from the mud of the Russian front to the sand of the Western Desert. This one is taking part in a mass surrender of German troops, who drove through British lines to give themselves up. The date was 3 May 1945, only five days before VE-day.**
(IWM)

The Magirus, Henschel and Krupp 6x4s were similar in general concept and size, although the Henschel 33D1 had a larger engine than most, at 10,857cc. Although out of production by 1938, thousands of these 6x4s saw service during the war. They were used for a variety of purposes, mainly load and personnel carrying, but also as signal vans, mobile offices, printing presses, workshop vehicles and ambulances.

An unusual design of 6x4 was the Krupp-Protze, powered by a 3308cc air-cooled flat-four engine, with a payload of 1150kg. It had coil spring independent suspension all round and a character-istic low, sloping bonnet made possible by the hor-izontal engine. It was made from 1934 to 1936 as the L2H43 with 55bhp engine, and from 1937 to 1941 as the L2H143 with engine uprated to 60bhp. It was used as a personnel carrier, searchlight truck, gun tractor and mobile telephone exchange.

Other 6x4s used by the Wehrmacht included the Austro Daimler ADGR 3 ton and Steyr 640 1½ ton from Austria and the Praga RV and Tatra 92 2 ton from Czechoslovakia. The latter had a 3980cc air-cooled V8 engine and was replaced in 1942 by the much larger Tatra 111, a remarkable machine with a payload of 6.3 tons, powered by a 14,825cc air-cooled V12 diesel engine. Like the smaller Tatra it had a central tubular backbone frame and inde-pendent suspension all round. This was one of the standard heavy trucks made under the Schell Programme and remained in production for many years after the war.

The Einheits Program initiated in 1936 envis-aged a standard range of trucks with two, three or

Above: **This Hansa-Lloyd 1½-ton truck was one of the countless civilian vehicles impressed into military service. It is being requisitioned by British airborne troops within five minutes of their landing near Hamminkeln, east of the Rhine, on 25 March 1945.** *(IWM)*

four axles, all driven and all independently sprung. Several prototypes were built, but only one design was made in quantity, the 2½-ton 6x6 which was described as a Leichter Geländegängiger Einheits Wehrmacht Lastwagen (Light Cross-Country Standard Army Truck). It was powered by a 6234cc six-cylinder diesel engine driving through a four-speed gearbox with two-speed auxiliary box. The lowest of the eight forward speeds available gave 3.5km/h, suitable for accompanying marching troops. Payload was 2500kg with open body and 2580kg with closed body. These 6x6 trucks were built by Büssing-NAG (3500), Henschel (1500), Magirus (2500) and MAN (1795) between 1937 and 1940. The engine was basically a MAN design and all development work was supervised by this company, while the chassis was the responsibility of Henschel. In addition to the standard load carrier, the Einheits 6x6 carried bodies for wireless, field telephone, tool storage, sound recording and surveying.

The Mittlerer Geländegängiger Einheits Wehrmacht Lastkraftwagen (Medium Cross-Country Standard Army Truck) was planned as an eight-wheeler, but went into production as a 6x4, made by Henschel and Magirus. It was based on the Henschel 33D1 which had appeared in 1933, and lacked the all-wheel drive and sophisticated suspension of the smaller Einheits trucks. About 3600 were made up to 1941.

The heavy Einheits design never got off the ground. Four prototypes were built by MAN in 1937/8, using modified 6x6 chassis with an additional driven axle behind the front one, and powered by a 120bhp V8 diesel engine. This 8x8 had originally been planned as a medium truck, but after a six-wheeled layout had been chosen for the 'Mittlerer Einheits,' the eight-wheeler was transferred to the heavy category, having a payload of 5 tons on roads and 4 tons cross-country. The four prototypes were subsequently converted to amphibians, in which form they used 150bhp six-cylinder engines.

As with the cars, the Einheits trucks were eliminated by the Schell plan, although of course they continued in service throughout the war. Under the Schell plan for trucks there were to be five categories, as follows, which were to replace all existing production vehicles:-

1 ton
1½ ton 4x2 and 4x4
3 ton 4x2 and 4x4
4½ ton 4x2 and 4 x4
6½ ton 6x4

For economy of production all these models had to be based on commercial models which could also be used for civilian purposes. This was an ironic reversal of the Nehring diktat that all motor production was to be subject to military demands, but

Right: **This Phänomen Granit survived well into the post-war era, and was photographed in Madrid in 1961. It was probably an ambulance originally, and may well have served with Germany's Condor Legion in the Spanish Civil War.**
(Nick Georgano)

the necessity for maximum possible output forced the decision. The only changes permitted to the basic civilian design were an increase in ground clearance, four-wheel drive and strengthening of chassis where necessary. This meant that the vehicles built under the Schell plan were of less technical interest than their predecessors, a contrast to the situation in Britain and America, where, as the war progressed, civilian trucks gave way to purpose built vehicles like the Bedford QL and GMC 6x6.

Only one design was built in the 1-ton category, the Borgward B1000, which was little changed from its civilian counterpart. In the 1½-ton class there were five manufacturers, Borgward, Daimler Benz, Opel, Phänomen and Steyr. Of these, the first three were available with 4x2 or 4x4 drive, and petrol or diesel engines in the case of the Borgward and Daimler Benz. The Phänomen Granit was made only in 4x2 form and was mainly used as an ambulance: it had an air-cooled 2678cc 50bhp petrol engine. The Steyr 1500 was made only as a 4x4 and used the same chassis as the Steyr command car described on page 86. The 3-ton was the largest class in terms of numbers made, with Opel alone turning out more than 95,000 and the total for all six makes being 183,129. The firms contributing to this total were Borgward, Daimler Benz, Ford, Magirus (now made by Klockner-Humboldt-Deutz), Opel and Stoewer. The Borgward was made in 4x2 and 4x4 forms, with petrol or diesel engines of 3745 and 4862cc respectively.

The 4x2 did not have a good reputation and a report from the Russian front said that on all the Borgwards in use the clutch slipped so badly that they could not be driven satisfactorily. The radiator pipes were too short and often came adrift on rough roads. The steering could hardly be moved under cold conditions. By contrast, the Opel Blitz (Lightning) 3 ton was highly praised in both 4x2

Left: **A Ford Lkw Type G 917 T, fitted with producer-gas equipment, manufactured between the years 1939-42.** *(Ford Motor Co)*

Left: **Typical of the 6x4 civilian trucks made during the 1930s and used in large numbers during the war is this Henschel with 10.8-litre 100bhp six-cylinder engine. A wide variety of bodies was built, including signals vans, mobile printing presses, workshops and fire engines.** *(Nick Baldwin Collection)*

and 4x4 versions. The Russian front report said that no faults had shown up in the 4x4 models and, of the trucks used in the desert, Opel and Ford were both said to have performed well, with Opel the better of the two. They were used for a variety of duties, with the Opel being particularly chosen as a tanker accompanying armoured units and taking hydrogen peroxide to rocket bases. The Ford was generally similar to the regular commercial model, powered by the 3.6-litre or 3.9-litre V8 engine, and was only made as a 4x2. Fords fitted with the larger engine had five-speed gearboxes, compared with four for the others. The earlier models had civilian type cabs, but as the war progressed they were turned out with a square cab, made of wood and compressed cardboard. A 4x4 open-cab variant was made in Hungary by the Mavag-Ford factory. There was also a semi-forward control 4x4 Ford (unusual at a time when German manufacturers were supposed to be standardising designs) which looked somewhat like a civilian American truck of 1940. Although some of these went to the Wehrmacht, more went to the Finnish Army for use in the war against Russia. It is said that, in return, the Finns had to hand over some 4x2 Ford trucks which they had aquired from America in 1940. Only 758 of the V3000A were made.

The 4½-ton trucks were made by Büssing-NAG, Daimler Benz and a consortium of OAF, Klockner-Humboldt-Deutz, MAN and Austrian Saurer. The Daimler Benz models 4500A and 4500S were also made by the Austrian firm Gräf & Stift. Each maker built two basic models, the 4500S 4x2 and the 4500A 4x4. The latter had transfer boxes which, in the case of the Mercedes-Benz, had two ratios giving a total of ten forward speeds. The Büssing and MAN transfer boxes served only to engage front-wheel drive and did not offer a change of ratio. The MAN and Mercedes-Benz trucks had spur gear reduction in their final drive, in the rims of the rear wheels but somewhat nearer the centre-line in the front axles.

The 6½ ton category were mostly six-wheelers, although Büssing-NAG made a four-wheeler in this class. They were made by Büssing-NAG, Vomag and a consortium of Faun, Fross-Büssing, Krupp and MAN who built trucks to a Faun design. They all had large six-cylinder engines (the Faun used a 150bhp 13,450cc Deutz diesel) and 6x4 drive. As well as for general duties, these six-wheelers were sometimes used for carrying light tanks. Numbers of Czech-built six-wheelers were also used by the Wehrmacht, including the Skoda ST6-T, with 100bhp six-cylinder engine, and two Tatra models, the 150bhp V8 model T81 and the 210bhp V12 model 111. The latter, which is described on page 93, was the only Czech truck to be built under the Schell plan, the others being pre-war designs carried on into the early war years.

Left: **The Phänomen Granit was a long-lived design which was first made in 1931 and continued in production into the early years of the war. It used the company's own make of 2.5-litre air-cooled engine and was made with Kübelwagen and ambulance bodies. One of the latter is seen here carrying German troops on their way to surrender, 2 May 1945.** *(IWM)*

In October 1943 a more drastic version of the Schell plan was laid down, in which truck types were restricted to a single 1½ ton (the Steyr 1500), two 3 ton (Ford and Mercedes-Benz), two 4½ ton (Büssing-NAG and Mercedes-Benz) and one 6½ ton (the Tatra 111). This plan also restricted car types to the VW Kübelwagen, which in theory had to suffice for everyone from line personnel to a Field Marshal. However, these constraints applied only to manufacture, not use, so the top brass still had access to their large Mercedes.

Ambulances

Several chassis were used by the Wehrmacht, of which the most common was the Phänomen Granit. This used an air-cooled four-cylinder, engine of 2497cc which had been introduced in 1931. The manufacturers were an old established company in Zittau, Saxony, who had won fame for their curious Phänomobil three-wheeler with engine mounted above the single front wheel, which they had made from 1907 to 1927. The Granit was used by many German towns as an ambulance and also by the Deutsche Reichspost as a combined mail and passenger vehicle. In 1936 it was adopted by the Army as an ambulance and first used on active service during the Spanish Civil War. It was also made with either an open or closed cab and could carry four stretchers or eight sitting patients. Maximum speed was around 50mph and on good surfaces the Granit was a satisfactory vehicle. However, its semi-elliptic springs gave a harsh ride over rough ground and it had poor traction in mud. To remedy the latter the makers introduced a

Above: **Apart from the Kettenrad, the smallest halftrack tractor was the Demag D7 (Sd.Kfz.10), rated as a 1-tonner. Powered by a 4.2-litre six-cylinder Maybach engine, it had a preselector gearbox with seven forward speeds and three reverse. Maximum speed on roads was about 40mph. This example is carrying a light anti-aircraft gun.** *(IWM)*

4x4 version called the Granit 1500A in 1940. This chassis was also used as a heavy command car or personnel carrier for the Afrika Corps. From 1943 onwards, the Granit 1500A (4x4) and 1500S (4x2) were the only ambulance models licenced for production under the revised Schell plan.

Other ambulances used in some numbers included the Adler W61K derived from the 3-litre six-cylinder Diplomat passenger car, of which about 500 were made from 1937 to 1939, and the Steyr 640 6x4 based on the maker's 1½-ton truck, of which 3,780 were built from 1937 to 1941. From 1940 onwards the Einheits Heavy Car as made by Horch was widely used for ambulance work. Mercedes-Benz and Opel Blitz truck chassis were also used with ambulance bodies, while heavier chassis by Ford, MAN, Opel and others were used as mobile operating theatres.

Heavy Tractors

Germany and Austria had a long tradition of making heavy road tractors, dating back to several years before World War One. Many of these were of advanced design, having four-wheel drive as early as 1905 on a prototype designed, or encouraged, by Archduke Leopold Salvator Hapsburg-Löthringen. In 1914 Austro Daimler put a 4x4 tractor into production, followed later in the war by German Daimler, Büssing and Magirus. Some of the German Daimlers were built for the Reichswehr up to the mid-1920s and in the following decade a new type of road tractor appeared. These had only two-wheel drive, being intended for high-speed towing on the new Autobahn network.

The best known makers of such tractors were Faun and Hanomag with Kaelble offering some slower moving machines particularly favoured by the Deutsche Reichsbahn (German State Railways), including a very advanced 6x6 tractor with 200bhp engine behind the cab. There were also a number of smaller tractors, based on agricultural versions but with full road equipment and different gearing, by such makers as Deuliwag, Deutz, Lanz and Normag. These were used as the lightest class of tractor by the Wehrmacht, while Hanomag made both medium and heavy tractors. The former

Right: **Among the heavy trucks of the Wehrmacht, the Büssing-NAG 4500S-1 was made in larger numbers than others, nearly 15,000 being turned out from 1942 to 1945. Several different bodies were used, including workshop vans and wreckers. They were powered by a 7.4-litre six-cylinder diesel engine.** *(School of Tank Technology)*

Below: **In appearance a standard Opel 3½-ton GS truck, this is in fact on a bus chassis, and carries a bus-type cab by Friedrich Rometsch of Berlin. It was used by the 15th Infantry supply column.** *(Vehicle displayed at the Victory Memorial Museum)*

had a 55bhp four-cylinder engine and weighed 4800kg. Top speed was 33mph, although it usually operated at a much lower speed. They were used by the Luftwaffe for towing aircraft and as refuelling trailers, as well as by the Wehrmacht for general duties.

Hanomag made several models of heavy tractor of which the SS100 was the best known. This had a 100bhp six-cylinder diesel engine and weighed 6540kg. It had a four-door double cab to carry a crew of five or six and could pull a drawbar trailer weighing up to 20 tons gross. Production of the SS100 lasted from 1936 to 1945 and a few later models, designated ST100, were made for the

French Army after the war. Hanomag road tractors of all sizes were popular as fairground transport well into the 1960s.

Faun also made a heavy tractor, powered by a 150bhp six-cylinder Deutz diesel engine of 13,540cc capacity. This was the largest and most powerful tractor available to the Wehrmacht. With four-door crew cab and a large ballast or tool box behind, it was more than 21 feet long and weighed 10,000kg. The road tractor model was known as the ZR and there was also the ZRS which was fitted with flanged wheels and buffers enabling it to operate on railway tracks.

The tractors so far described were used for general transport and, to a limited extent, for pulling low loading tank-carrying trailers. However, on the whole the Wehrmacht preferred to transport their tanks by rail. For artillery tractors they used the halftrack tractors described in the next section. Here also will be found the only wheeled artillery tractors made for the Wehrmacht, the Latil FTARH and the Skoda Radschlepper Ost, for these were closer to the halftracks in function, if not in appearance.

Halftracks

Germany produced a greater number of halftrack vehicles than any other nation, and they played a great part in the successful Blitzkrieg attacks on Poland, France and the Netherlands in the first nine months of the war. Experiments had begun with this type of vehicle in 1917 when Benz built a medium semi-tracked tractor, and a few designs appeared sporadically during the 1920s. Daimler Benz produced the Mercedes-Benz ZD5 in 1931. This was a 12-seater personnel carrier with solid rubber tyres at the front. It was intended for the Russian government, but they took few, if any, and in the absence of other orders the project lapsed. It was only with the massive rearmament programme ordered by the Nazi government that halftracks began to be made in numbers, and this was well under way by 1936. Eventually a whole range would be built, mostly to a standardised design, from the motorcycle-like NSU Kettenkrad with

single front wheel, 9ft long and weighing 1235kg, to the Famo Zugkraftwagen, 27 feet long and weighing 15,470kg empty.

The halftracks were collectively known as Sd. Kfz (Sonderkraft-fahrzeug - special motor vehicle) with the tractor models bearing the additional title Zgkw (Zugkraftwagen – train motor vehicle). They all had needle roller bearing tracks with detachable rubber track pads, torsion bar suspension on all but the front wheels (except on early 8 ton models), large double and overlapping bogie wheels, and steering by Cletrac-type varied track speed as well as by the front wheels. Apart from the Opel-powered NSU Kettenkrad, all halftracks used Maybach engines, varying from a 90bhp six-cylinder to a 230bhp V12. Like the other Einheits models, they were made in three standard sizes; light, medium and heavy.

The Kettenkrad was a most unusual vehicle, the like of which was never seen in any other army. It resembled a motorcycle only in its single front wheel, forks and handlebars, for the driver's saddle was enclosed by bodywork which extended for the rest of the vehicle and was carried on two substantial tracks. Two crew members sat facing rearwards, over the 1478cc four-cylinder Opel Olympia engine. Two side facing radiators, between driver and passengers, provided cooling, and in very cold climates warm air from the engine could be directed towards the driver. The Kettenkrad had two means of steering, by handlebars on the front wheel for gentle curves, or by varying the speed of the tracks for more radical change of direction at low speeds. A top speed of 50mph was claimed, but

Above: **Phänomen Werke of Zittau made a speciality of air-cooled engines, which had the advantage in extreme climates of being unable to freeze or boil. As well as the older-style 4x2 ambulances (see page 77), Phänomen made 4x4 chassis used as light trucks and ambulances. This is the command car (Kfz.70) with desert tyres.**
(Bart Vanderveen Collection)

the Kettenkrad was virtually unmanageable at anything over 40mph and, as it was normally used for towing, its ordinary speed was much lower. Thanks to its traction it could tow loads of up to 4 tons on level ground. Total production of Kettenkrads was 8345 (by NSU and Stoewer), and most were used, and subsequently abandoned, on the Russian Front. A few survived the war to be used as forestry tractors in Germany.

Design and manufacture of the various types of halftrack was as follows, with one company being allocated overall responsibility for design and development, although production was often farmed out to other firms as well.

LIGHT
½ ton Sd Kfz NSU
36bhp Opel four-cylinder engine

1 ton Sd Kfz 10 Demag
90bhp Maybach (55bhp BMW 319 on earliest examples)

3 ton Sd Kfz 11 Hanomag
90bhp Maybach six-cylinder

3 ton Sd Kfz 11 HansaLloyd
90bhp Maybach six-cylinder

MEDIUM
5 ton Sd Kfz 6 Büssing-NAG
100bhp Maybach six-cylinder

8 ton Sd Kfz 7 Krauss-Maffei
115 or 140bhp Maybach six-cylinder

HEAVY
12 ton Sd Kfz 8 Mercedes-Benz
185bhp Maybach V12

18 ton Sd Kfz 9 Famo
230bhp Maybach V12

Manufacturers to whom production was subcontracted included Adler, Büssing-NAG, Phänomen, Saurer and Skoda (light), Praga and Tatra (medium), and Krauss-Maffei, Krupp, Skoda and Tatra (heavy). The weight indicates towing capacity rather than payload, as they were essentially towing vehicles rather than load carriers. The great majority, in all classes, were artillery tractors, although the smaller models were used as eight-seater personnel carriers in the Blitzkrieg campaigns. Some of these were armoured and carried two machine guns, two machine carbines and flame throwers. The medium and heavy halftracks sometimes carried anti-aircraft guns, a typical mounting on the 18-ton Famo being an 88mm Flak (*Flieger abwehr kanone*) anti-aircraft gun. As a tractor, the Mercedes-Benz DB9

carried a crew of 13. The Famo F2/3 was often used for tank recovery, being equipped with a manually operated or petrol-electric crane. Almost 100,000 halftracks were made in Germany between 1934 and 1945, while Krauss-Maffei assembled a few more from existing parts for the British Army in 1946.

The last halftrack was a simplified design, more in keeping with the philosophy of the Schell plan. This was known as the S.WS (Schwere Wehrmachtschlepper – heavy army tractor) and had a simpler body and tracks than the preceding series. Made by Bussing and Tatra only, the S.WS was powered by a 100bhp Maybach six-cylinder engine similar to that used in the last Maybach SW42 passenger cars. Braking was by an air-actuated Argus disc brake on the transmission. Most of the 1000 or so made between December 1943 and March 1945 carried armoured bodywork, but about 175 were soft skinned.

Despite their good showing at the beginning of the war, the halftracks turned out to be a mixed blessing. The machines which had roared over the flat terrain and relatively good roads of Eastern France and Belgium in 1940 did not perform so heroically in the mud and ice of the Russian campaign eighteen months later. They required complex maintenance, including greasing 110 individual track pins at regular intervals. Even if this was adhered to, and often it was not, the tractors had a combat life of less than two years, and they

were extremely expensive to replace. The high grade steel required for the needle rollers (80 per track pin) was in very short supply. In November 1941 a directive came from Hitler himself that a cheaper form of artillery tractor must be developed with all speed.

Specifications were issued for two types, the Radschlepper Ost (Wheeled Tractor, East) and the Raupenschlepper Ost (Tracked Tractor, East). Development of the former was entrusted to the celebrated engineer Dr Ferdinand Porsche: Hitler had a high personal regard for Porsche who had produced the Volkswagen for him, and it had not been forgotten that Porsche had designed some very advanced 4x4 tractors for Austro-Daimler during World War One. Porsche went to work and came up with a curious looking machine, riding high on its 1500mm wheels and looking very like an updated version of the 1914 Austro-Daimler. It was powered by a 90bhp 6024cc four-cylinder petrol engine mounted under a large forward-projecting bonnet. To aid starting under extremely cold conditions, an auxiliary engine was provided; this consisted of two cylinders of Volkswagen engine, and was mounted beside the front of the main engine. Its purpose was to pre-heat the latter's inlet manifold, cylinders and lubricating oil, to act as a starter, and, as a useful by-product, to heat the driver's cab. Transmission was by a five-speed gearbox, with a single-speed transfer box providing

drive to the front and rear axles. The wheels were shod with iron tyres, partly to save rubber and also because Hitler had been impressed with the performance of iron tyres on the World War One artillery tractors of the Austrian Army.

In October 1942, barely seven months after Porsche had been charged with the job of producing the Radschlepper Ost, the first prototype was ready. They and subsequent production models were made in the Skoda factory, as indeed the 1914/18 Austro Daimlers had been. In January 1943 Hitler attended a demonstration of the Porsche tractor together with the French-built Latil FTARH which was a similar concept. Neither performed very well, and the Führer promptly reduced the initial order for 200 to 100. The metal wheels were not wide enough to provide traction in deep mud, while on inclined smooth surfaces they simply spun. Also they transmitted very uncomfortable vibration to the driver's compartment. It is likely that few ever saw service on the Russian Front for which they were intended, but a number went to Western Europe where they were used in France and Holland. The number made is unknown, but it may not have been very much more than the initial 100.

Instead of the Radschlepper Ost the Wehrmacht used halftrack versions of four Schell plan trucks - the 2-ton Opel Blitz, 3-ton Ford and Klockner-

Humboldt-Deutz, and 4½-ton Mercedes-Benz. These were not only effective tractors but also carried a useful load. About 300 Opels were fitted with armour and a ten-barrel rocket launcher. These halftrack trucks were collectively called Maultier (Mule) and were made in considerable numbers – nearly 14,000 Fords, 4,000 Opels, 2,500 Klockner-Humbolt-Deutz (K-H-D) and 1480 Mercedes-Benz.

The other truck intended specifically for the Eastern front, the full-track Raupenschlepper Ost, was designed and built by the Austrian Steyr company, and also made under contract by Gräf & Stift in Austria and by Auto Union and Klockner-Humboldt-Deutz in Germany. It was powered by a 3517cc air-cooled V8 engine, the same unit that powered the Steyr 1500 command car and light truck, and had a four-speed transmission. The original version (RSO/01) had an enclosed cab with side windows and doors, but the later RSO/03, built by K-H-D, had an open soft-top cab and used a Deutz diesel engine. The main purpose of the RSO was as a gun tractor, but it had a truck body which could carry loads up to 1½ tons, and could also carry an SP gun. Other applications included a snow plough, ambulance, anti-tank gun carrier, amphibian and tractor for use with a tracked semi-trailer. Top speed was no more than 10mph, which at least put relatively little strain on the transmission

and tracks. Steering was by applying the front and rear track brakes on either side, and was not very effective. More than 27,000 RSOs were made between 1942 and 1945, the greatest single producer being the Magirus-Deutz factory at Cologne, which built about 12,520. K-H-D made a few halftrack versions just after the war, with shortened track bogies and a front axle under the cab. Presumably assembled from parts already to hand, they were called Waldschlepper (forest tractor). Considering the large number of RSOs made (some sources claim as many as 28,257), hardly any have survived, though three are in the hands of a Belgian collector, Guy Franz Arend of the Victory Memorial Museum. Many were destroyed by their crews before being abandoned in the later stages of the war.

Other full-track vehicles included two artillery tractors made by Praga, the six-cylinder T3 and V8 T9, and an amphibious tractor designed by Rheinmetall-Borsig and built by a consortium including Alkett GmbH of Spandau, Sachsenberg AG of Dessau and Hattenwerke of Southofen. It was powered by a 300bhp Maybach V12 engine and had twin-propeller drive for water use, where it served as a tug for boats. It could also be launched from a landing craft and might have seen service in this role had the planned invasion of Britain ever taken place. Only 21 of these Land-Wasser-Schlepper (Land-Water-Tractor) were made.

CHAPTER FOUR

United States

Military purchases rose dramatically,
from about 46,000 vehicles in 1939/40 to 62,258
in the one month of June 1942.

The contribution of the United States vehicle industry to the Allied war effort cannot be overestimated – not only did it provide mobility for American forces in all theatres of the war, but through the Lend-Lease Programme vast numbers of wheeled and tracked vehicles were supplied to Great Britain and the USSR. More than 400,000 vehicles went to the Soviets, and the total value of the goods provided under Lend-Lease was in excess of 42 billion dollars.

This tremendous production effort was all the more remarkable as up to the mid-1930s the US military vehicle fleet was very ancient, as America had ended the First World War with a large number of serviceable vehicles, some of which were gradually modernised in the 1920s by the replacement of solid tyres with pneumatics, enclosing cabs and so on. With no conflict on the horizon to justify spending on new vehicles, hardly any were bought: from the end of the war up to June 1929 the Quartermaster Corps purchased only 763 new vehicles, of which 709 were staff cars. This meant that the armed forces of the leading industrial nation in the world bought precisely 54 new trucks in ten years!

In 1931 the Quartermaster Corps pressed for some degree of standardisation of trucks, and where suitable civilian models could not be bought for the right price, they began a policy of assembling their own. This took place at Fort Holabird, Maryland, and followed an experimental test period when 6x6 versions of Liberty trucks had been manufactured.

The QMC trucks, as they were called, ranged from 1¼ to 12 tons in rated capacity, came in 4x2, 4x4, 6x4 and 6x6 models, and included fuel tankers and fire engines. Engines were purchased from Continental, Franklin, Hercules, Lycoming and Sterling, and other well-known proprietary components were used, such as Spicer gearboxes, Rockwell axles, Ross steering etc. One such truck, a 2½-ton 6x6 high speed truck of which at least two were made, used the 6.9-litre twin-ohc straight-eight Duesenberg engine.

Most of the trucks were handsome, up-to-date vehicles with chromed radiator shells which resembled those of the later Marmon-Herrington. Not surprising, as Arthur W. Herrington worked at Fort Holabird before he formed the Indianapolis company with Walter Marmon.

The first QMC trucks were built in 1932, and the programme seemed to have a bright future. So bright in fact that it alarmed the commercial truck makers who were looking forward to fat Army contracts when the fifteen-year-old Libertys and Whites finally wore out. The manufacturers applied pressure on Congress to stop any further development on production of QMC vehicles, and before the beginning of 1933 Fort Holabird resumed its former role as an evaluator of military equipment. About 60 QMC trucks were made, and most survived up to the war period, although they were not used for combat purposes.

In 1934 Congress passed the War Department Appropriation Act which forbade the use of army

funds to repair or modernise pre-1920 vehicles, as from 1 January 1935. This was the first step towards eliminating the ancients, and led to large orders being placed for up-to-date vehicles. These were mostly slightly modified commercial models, and it was not until 1939 that a standardisation programme was laid down, which led to the development of many of the most familiar American trucks of World War Two, such as the ¾-ton 4x4 Dodge and the 2½-ton 6x6 GMC. Five main types were standardised at first, at ½, 1½, 2½, 4 and 7½ tons, but the ½ ton was later uprated to ¾ ton and eventually 1 ton, and larger categories added up to 10 tons. Military purchases rose dramatically, from about 46,000 vehicles in 1939/40 to 62,258 in the one month of June 1942. These figures are for the US forces only, and do not take into account the vast numbers of vehicles (as well as aircraft and other equipment) supplied under the Lend-Lease Programme.

At the outbreak of war America was still following a strictly neutral foreign policy, and there was an embargo on the supply of weapons to any of the warring nations. Within ten days of the British and French declaration of war on Germany however, President Roosevelt called a special session of Congress to reconsider the embargo, and after much discussion the embargo was lifted in November 1939. Interestingly, in view of America's wholehearted commitment to the war later on, the decision was by no means unanimous, the voting being 63 to 30 in the Senate, and 245 to 181 in the House of Representatives.

At first all equipment was bought outright by both British and French purchasing commissions; after the fall of France in June 1940, the French contracts were taken over by the British. It soon emerged that Britain lacked the dollars to continue high-level purchasing , and by the end of 1940 they were obliged to suspend their orders. Winston Churchill set out the stark position in a letter to President Roosevelt dated 8 December 1940, which he afterwards described as one of the most important letters he had ever written. In a broadcast of 9 February 1941 he included the famous words "Give us the tools and we will finish the job," to which the Lend-Lease Bill was a direct response.

Rather than make long-term loans, the repayment of which had caused a lot of trouble after World War One, the US Government decided to invoke a law of 1892 which allowed the Defence Secretary to lend material not considered essential to the army for a period of not more than five years. Those who drafted the original law could never have envisaged the manner in which it would be applied 49 years later, but it was an ingenious solution to the problem, said to have been worked out by the Treasury with the wholehearted approval of President Roosevelt.

The Lend-Lease Bill was signed by the President on 11 March 1941, and an initial budget of seven billion dollars was approved. Britain and Greece were the first recipients, followed by China. After the German attack on Russia in June 1941 America had to revise its attitude to the Soviet

Above: **An M2 or M3 personnel carrier with troops leaping into action, probably a publicity shot taken in America rather than in the heat of battle. White built the greater number of this standardised design, also made by Autocar, Diamond T and International. The White-built chassis were driven from Cleveland to Canton, Ohio, about 60 miles to the south, to be fitted with bodies by the Diebold Safe & Lock Company. The 120-mile round trip, with mainly female drivers, was a useful running-in period, after which the halftracks were sent by railway to ports for shipment to the war zones.**

Right: **King George VI inspects a Bantam-BRC with anti-aircraft machine gun.** *(The Tank Museum, Bovington)*

Right: **King George VI inspects a Bantam-BRC with anti-aircraft machine gun.** *(The Tank Museum, Bovington)*

Below: **A White M3A1 scout car with the Field Regiment Signals Section of the Royal Artillery. It is equipped with a Canadian wireless set No.52 and a wireless set No.19; the first was for controlling the Command Net (the main group of wireless stations in the regiment), and the second was for the rear link to divisional HQ.** *(IWM)*

Union; at first trucks and other equipment were supplied against payment of cash and goods, but in June 1942 the Lend-Lease Bill was extended to the Soviet Union. In 1943 alone, Russia received from the USA 210,000 vehicles, 3,734 tanks and two million tyres. Nevertheless Britain was the largest beneficiary of Lend-Lease, receiving 42% of the total, with 28% going to Russia, and the balance to New Zealand, Australia, China, Brazil, and, as aid to reconstruction after the countries were liberated, to France, Holland, Norway and Poland. When the vehicles used by America's own armed forces are added to the Lend Lease figures, one reaches the formidable total of 3,200,436 transport vehicles, 88,410 tanks, and 41,170 tracked vehicles.

Staff Cars

The staff car did not get off to a very good start in the US Army. One was offered to General Fred G. Grant during the Pennsylvania Manoeuvres of 1906, but he refused to ride in it, saying that it would not do for him to appear before his subordinates unless he was mounted on his horse! Other generals were not so choosy, however, and the open touring car became an accepted form of transport for senior officers, joined by saloons and limousines during World War One.

Four basic types of staff car were in use during World War Two, five- and seven-passenger sedans, and five- and seven-passenger station wagons. They were all little-modified civilian types, though some of the station wagons had large section tyres, 9x13ins compared with the normal 6x16ins. Other modifications included blackout lighting: 1941 Fords had their stylised sidelights, which were above the headlights, replaced by little bullet-

Above: **Long wheelbase Jeeps were made in wheeled 6x6 form and as halftracks. They were largely experimental.**
(The Tank Museum, Bovington)

Left: **A Jeep with wheelbase extended by 3 ft, beside a standard model. This ten-seater was operated by US Coast Guardsmen, and possibly built by them. Certainly some lwb Jeeps were built in Europe from two damaged vehicles.**
(IWM)

Above: **A Jeep speeding from a landing barge onto the beach at Hollandia, New Guinea, during the successful attack by US troops on the Japanese-held base. Large numbers of troops await disembark-ation from the landing craft in the background.**
(IWM)

Right: **One of the pre-production prototypes of the Bantam Jeep, in service with the Canadian Army, photographed in Windsor, Ontario, in 1941.**
(Public Archives of Canadian)

shaped blackout lights which became the sole means of lighting. Plymouths had sidelights as part of the headlight assembly, so had the bullet shaped lights added. Vehicles used in Britain had to conform with local regulations, and were fitted with the familiar headlight masks. The five-passenger sedans were mostly the low priced 'Big Three' makes, Chevrolet, Ford and Plymouth, 1940 to 1942 models.

Production of the latter was halted in February 1942, and dealers' stocks frozen until they should be needed by the Army. The decisions to utilise these stocks was made in November 1942, and 29,000 more sedans joined the Army, the last new cars to do so until after the war.

Larger cars used by the forces included Buicks, Oldsmobiles, Packards and Cadillacs. General Eisenhower used a Packard Clipper sedan for much of the war, supplemented by a 1942 Cadillac Series 75 limousine. In London his chauffeur was an English girl, Kay Summersby, with whom he fell in love and might have married after the war had not he received the sternest discouragement from General Marshall, the United States Chief of Staff. General Douglas MacArthur used a 1941 Cadillac at his HQ in Manila from where he masterminded the Pacific campaign. General George S. Patton used a 1939-style Cadillac limousine which was in fact assembled in France in 1945 from parts shipped over from the US. In December 1945 he was riding in this car in Mannheim when it was in collision with a GMC truck; the General received injuries from which he died twelve days later. The car was repaired, and can now be seen at the Patton Museum at Fort Knox,

Above and left:
One of the 1642 Bantam-built BRC Jeeps, fitted with a Browning M2 machine gun.
(The Tank Museum, Bovington)

Right: **A Jeep ambulance carrying three British soldiers wounded during the storming of the River Orne and the battle for Caen, July 1944.** *(IWM)*

Below: **Lieutenant General B.L. Montgomery, as he was in May 1942, when GOC South Eastern Command. He is riding in a Jeep during an exercise in Kent.** *(IWM)*

Kentucky. Senior officers' cars carried a plaque at the front indicating their occupants' status – the Patton Cadillac had a four-star plaque, MacArthur's a five star.

Scout Cars

The concept of a light car with good cross-country mobility that could gather information near the front line appeared very early in American military circles. In 1898 Colonel Royal P. Davidson adapted a three-wheeled Duryea car to carry a 0.45 calibre Colt Model 1895 machine gun and a small amount of armour plate. He followed this with three four-wheelers, two of them steam-powered, while various adaptations of passenger cars were used in Mexico against Pancho Villa's forces in 1916. Light, open four-seaters based on Ford and Chevrolet chassis were made experimentally in the 1920s and 1930s, and the ancestors of the World War Two scout cars appeared in the mid-1930s.

In 1934 the White Motor Company of Cleveland, Ohio, developed a purpose-built reconnaissance car based on the 1½-ton 4x4 commercial chassis built by their subsidiary, Indiana Motors

Corporation. It had a 4.6-litre 75bhp six-cylinder Hercules engine, Brown-Lipe gearbox and Wisconsin transfer box. On this chassis was built a body with shoulder-high armour at the side and armoured protection for the radiator. It also had three mountings for machine guns. It was given the name T7 or M1, and was the ancestor of a line of White-built scout cars made up to 1944.

In September 1937 came the M2A1 with a 5.2-litre 95bhp Hercules engine and lower lines. This became the M3 and finally in 1939 the M3A1 with engine up-rated to 110bhp. This had a wider body than its predecessors, and could carry a 0.50 Browning M2 machine gun at the front, and two 0.30 Browning A4s at the sides. To prevent the front bumper from embedding itself in soft ground, the M3A1 had a roller mounted ahead of the bumper. It proved very satisfactory for escort or security operations but its lack of comprehensive armour prevented it from being suitable in combat operations. Most M3A1s had a canvas topped rear body, and in order to reduce weight the armoured sides were not as high as those of the original Indiana M1. A total of 20,918 M3A1s were made in five years, and they were used by Canadian, British and Russian forces as well as by the US Army.

Above: **A Dodge T214 command car was used by the Soviet Marshal Zhukov when he inspected the 82nd US Airborne Division at Berlin's Tempelhof Aerodrome on 31 August 1945.** *(IWM)*

Right: **The WC54 was the most popular ambulance on the Dodge T214; 26,000 were made between 1942 and 1944. They could accomodate four stretcher cases or seven sitting patients.**
(J Spencer-Smith)

Below: **Two contrasting types of ambulance in service with the US army just before America's entry into the war in December 1941. On the left is a field ambulance based on a 1934 Chevrolet panel van, and to the right an urban-type ambulance, a 1941 Cadillac with a body by Superior Coach Corporation of Lima, Ohio.**
(Fred Crismon Collection)

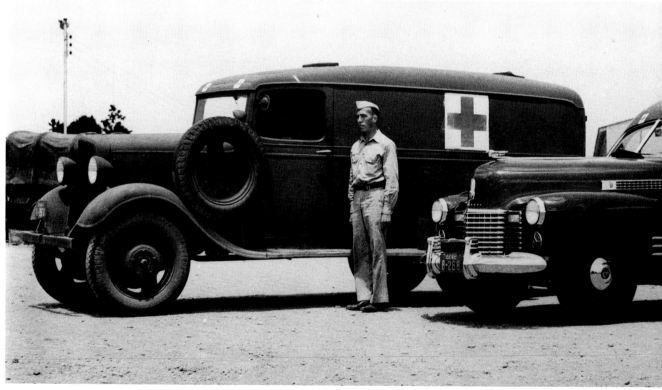

Left: **The Linn Multiplant ambulance could carry 12 stretchers. This early model was powered by a Dodge six-cylinder engine, but a Mercury V8 replaced it on later Linns. Drive was to the front wheels which allowed for a flat floor area in which operations could be performed.** *(Fred Crismon Collection)*

The Canadians described the White as a 15cwt armoured truck rather than as a scout car. It was also used as a six-passenger personnel carrier and as an ambulance. From it was developed the larger and more powerful M3 halftrack made by White, Diamond T, Autocar and International (see page 111).

A contemporary of the M1 was the Corbitt M2E1, similar in concept and also based on a 1½-ton truck chassis. It had a 4.6-litre eight-cylinder Lycoming engine, and a road speed of 50mph.

Only twenty were made, and none saw active service. The only other vehicle of this period in the armoured scout car class were Jeeps, described on page 125.

Ambulances

Ambulances used during World War Two fell into two main categories, 'metropolitan' vehicles with 4x2 drive and only suitable for areas with well surfaced roads, and 'tactical' or field ambulances intended to take the wounded from the front line to a field hospital.

In the former category were numerous civilian type ambulances and in America these were based on passenger car chassis, whereas in Britain they tended to be based on light commercial vehicles. There were several specialist builders of ambulances in America, of which Henney, Hess & Eisenhart and Superior Coach were among the best known. Their normal practice was to take a high quality chassis such as a Cadillac or Packard, lengthen the wheelbase by one or two feet, and build on it a rear-loading, four-stretcher ambulance body. The result was sleek, comfortable and fast, ideally suited to city work, but for rescue work in the field something more rugged was needed. In the 1930s the best available field ambulances were 1½-ton vans by Ford and Chevrolet. Most of these had twin rear wheels and reasonable ground clearance, but their lack of four-wheel drive made them unsuitable for really rough work.

Fortunately, by the time America entered the war new purpose-built 4x4 chassis were available. The Jeep was widely used as a two- or three-

Below: **The 3-ton VK62B was Dodge's heaviest truck in the 1939/40 era. Basically a civilian model, this army version has a Gar Wood all-steel body, radiator guard and tow hooks. In 1944 the VK62B was suceeded by the T234 with military front end but the same engine and gearbox.** *(NMM)*

stretcher field ambulance, while the ¾-ton Dodge was also very popular for longer journeys. The White M3A1 scout car was also used for ambulance work but was not very satisfactory as it had no opening at the back, and stretchers had to be lifted over the high sides. These 4x4 are described in their relevant sections.

An unusual vehicle which was more of a mobile emergency hospital than an ambulance was the Linn, made by the Linn Coach & Truck Company of Oneonta, New York. This was based on the vans which the company had made for the civilian market, particularly as travelling showrooms. They were 28ft 8ins long and 7ft 6ins high, which provided an adequate working area for surgical operations. Five or more could be used in conjunction with a large tent to provide a sizeable Mobile Army Surgical Hospital, of the kind immortalised in the television series MASH. Alas, the latter did not feature Linns, of which only 25 were made. They were powered by Mercury V8 engines driving the front wheels, and had a road speed of 50mph.

Trucks, ¼ ton 4x4

Although the four-passenger Jeep might be thought of as a car, it was always classified by the US Army as a light truck. In the Canadian and British Armies it was called a 'Car, 5cwt, 4x4'. It was conceived by the Quartermaster Corps who wanted a lighter 4x4 than the ½-tonner made by Marmon-Herrington and Dodge (see page 128). In June 1940 they laid down specifications for a 4x4 vehicle to carry 500 pounds, to weigh no more than 1300 pounds, with an engine of at least 40bhp.

The American Bantam Co of Butler, Pennsylvania, who had been making an Americanised version of the Austin Seven, had supplied some of their vehicles to the Army and hoped to tender for the new light truck contract. However the stipulation of a 40hp engine was fatal to their hopes of basing it on the Bantam, which developed no more than 20bhp. If they were to make a bid, Bantam would have to produce a completely new design, and their President, Frank Finn, called in an experienced design consultant, Karl K. Probst. He took up his new post on 17 July 1940, with the responsibility of producing a running prototype within 49 days of receiving the contract. The actual design work took 18 hours, and the plans were submitted to the Army at Fort Holabird on 22 July. Bantam was the only company to promise to keep to the Army's 49 day limit (Willys could not do better than 75 days) so the Butler firm received the contract, which was delivered on 1 August. They met the deadline, and

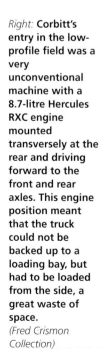

Right: **Corbitt's entry in the low-profile field was a very unconventional machine with a 8.7-litre Hercules RXC engine mounted transversely at the rear and driving forward to the front and rear axles. This engine position meant that the truck could not be backed up to a loading bay, but had to be loaded from the side, a great waste of space.**
(Fred Crismon Collection)

the prototype BRC (Bantam Reconnaissance Command) was driven throught the gates of Fort Holabird on 22 September.

The engine was a 45bhp 1.8-litre four-cylinder Continental. Spicer axles, which were made for the Studebaker Champion car, and a Spicer transfer box were also fitted. The open four-passenger body was very similar to that adopted on subsequent models. The only part of the specification which Probst and his team failed to deliver was the weight limit – the BRC turned the scales at 1850 pounds, but the Army accepted this, partly because a General was able to lift it from the rear by himself. Production cars with additional equipment weighed 2000 pounds.

The BRC performed impressively, and Bantam received an initial order for 70, which were delivered in December 1940. Eight of these had rear-wheel steering, but this did not prove satisfactory. According to Probst the theory behind it was that, in the event of danger ahead "the driver was to ram the car into reverse and pour on the power, releasing the steering wheel. The man in the back would use the tiller to steer them out of ambush."

In January 1941 Ford delivered the first of their version, which was powered by a 42bhp 1.9-litre four-cylinder tractor engine, but in every other respect looked very similar to the Willys or later Bantam BRC. They built 1500 pilot models, called the GP (G-Government, suffix-P), and, once they had got the weight down, Willys made a similar number of their MA models.

Army trials continued through the spring of 1941, and in July they asked for bids to produce

16,000 vehicles at the rate of 125 a day. The small Bantam plant had a maximum capacity of 40 per day, so although they had done all the pioneering work and had met the original deadline, they had to drop out. In all they made 2,642 BRCs, and spent the rest of the war making two-wheeled trailers to be towed behind Ford or Willys Jeeps.

It was during the shake-down period before large-scale production got under way that the new vehicle received its name. The Ford GP was just asking to be contracted to Jeep, perhaps encouraged by the existence of a well known cartoon character called 'the jeep', but the name would probably have been coined anyway. It was first used in print by *The Washington Post* on 16 March 1941, and soon became the universal name, though never officially adopted by Ford, and not by Willys until after the war. Some people thought it should be called the Peep (because it was a reconnaissance vehicle), and in November 1942 *The Motor* ran an article "Peeps Under Test" in which they said that the name Jeep was given to a larger four-wheel-drive vehicle, by which they presumably meant the ¹/₂-ton Dodge. However no one subscribed to this idea for long, and indeed the very next week *The Autocar* stated "…to refer to a Jeep as a Peep in the hearing of an American soldier is to make a *faux pas.*"

Having received the contract for mass production, Willys set out to refine their Jeep, the new model appearing at the end of 1941 as the MB. In appearance the chief difference was that the radiator tank bearing the name Willys, embossed in letters three inches high, was concealed by an extension of the slatted grille, so that the MB bore

Right: **The Studebaker model LC low-profile truck was even weirder than the Corbitt, and looked more like a trailer than a powered truck, with its 3.8-litre Hercules JXD engine mounted outboard between the wheels on the right-hand side.**
(Fred Crismon Collection)

no name at all. Also the headlights, which were mounted above the wings on the MA, were integrated into the sides of the grille. Pivoted lights, which could be swung up and over to illuminate the engine during night repairs, were introduced on the Ford Jeep and quickly adopted by Willys. These were fitted on all Jeeps manufactured up to 1945.

The engine was the 2.2-litre 54bhp side-valve which had been used to power Willys passenger cars since 1933. Drive was through a three-speed gearbox with synchromesh on second and top, with a two-speed transfer box. Brakes were hydraulic, and top speed was about 65mph, although the ride at that speed was so bumpy that it was seldom maintained for long.

Above: **The driver sat low and almost in the centre, with entry into the 'cab' by the ring steps mounted below the front members.**
(Fred Crismon Collection)

Right: **The weight of the engine was matched by a 60-gallon fuel-tank on the left-hand side.**
(Fred Crismon Collection)

The Willys MB went into production in December 1941, and was followed a month or two later by Ford GPW (General Purpose Willys). As the Willys design proved to be the most satisfactory, with nearly 30% more power, it was adopted for production by Ford, although minor differences existed between the two makes. For example the Ford's front chassis cross-member was an inverted U-section, while the Willys's was tubular.

In order to take advantage of the greater standardisation, the US Army took many of the MB/GPW models, while the earlier Bantam BRC, Ford GP and Willys MA went via Lend-Lease to Britain and the Soviet Union. Total production of the standardised Jeep between December 1941 and the summer of 1945 reached the remarkable figure of 639,245, of which 277,896 were Ford-built GPWs and 361,349 Willys MBs. From 1942 to 1945 bodies for the Willys Jeep were made by the American Central Manufacturing Corp of Connersville, Indiana, descended from the company which had made Auburn and Cord cars. American Central also supplied about 50,000 bodies to Ford – probably to the latter's plant at Louisville, Kentucky, which was the nearest Ford plant to Connersville.

Although there were a number of experimental variations, the basic Jeep underwent little change during the war. They were used for personnel carrying, as ambulances with one or two 'decks' of stretchers, and as mounts for 37mm self-propelled guns. There was even a 6x6 version, made by Willys, for carrying the 37mm gun. There was also an armoured version, and the 6x6 could be used as a tractor with semi-trailers for cargo carrying and

ambulance work. These tractors were air portable. The 6x6s had 100-inch wheelbases, 20 inches longer than the regular Jeep.

For ambulance work the spare wheel was sometimes removed from its usual position at the back of the body, and repositioned between the stretchers, just behind the driver. The record for a Jeep ambulance was seven stretchers, two behind the driver, three on a platform above, and two transversely over the bonnet.

Specialised adaptations of Jeeps included roadrailers with flanged wheels for travelling on the empty railways of Western Europe after the Liberation, and armoured scout cars. The latter were specially prepared by the Smart Engineering Co. of Detroit.

The first, made in 1941, had armour over the radiator and bonnet, and an armoured windscreen of the same shape and size as an ordinary Jeep, but later versions had a lower profile with a sharply sloping screen and better protection at the sides. The drawback was that as the Jeep became safer, the weight increased, and the final Smart-armoured Jeep carried more than 1000 pounds of armour in addition to its regular weight of about 2000 pounds.

Among the most unusual Jeep adaptations were an autogiro version modified by the Australians for use in New Guinea, and a mock Kübelwagen in which the 'driver' was a dummy and the vehicle was actually controlled from the rear seat. Its short wheelbase would have given the game away to any experienced observer.

Although usually thought of as a fairly humble means of transport, the Jeep carried Generals from

Left: **The Dodge WC17 Carryall was a hybrid vehicle, using the body of the civilian Suburban with militarised front end and bonnet. It was rated for ${}^1\!/_2$ ton loads, and in 1942 gave way to the lower and wider T 214 which was rated as a ${}^3\!/_4$ tonner.**
(The Tank Museum, Bovington)

time to time. Field Marshal Montgomery was not above riding in a Jeep, and General Patton had one with a curious home-made saloon body. Field Marshal Rommel admired the Jeep, and during the North African and Italian campaigns ordered that captured Jeeps should be used for combat duties in preference to German vehicles, which should be relegated to support work.

The small size of the Jeep made it ideal for use in landing craft, and it could be carried in much smaller boats than heavy trucks. It was also airportable, while large numbers were sent across the Atlantic in PKD (Partly Knocked Down) or CKD (Completely Knocked Down) form. Those sent to Britain were assembled in factories or garages, but in France an 'assembly line' was often set up in a field which had been vacated by cows only an hour or so before. The crates were taken by mobile crane from the beaches, where the landing ships had left them, to the fields where they were set out in appropriate places. The chassis was lifted out of its

crate by a Diamond T Wrecker, and the wheels put on while it was still 'airborne.' It was then lowered to the ground, and the other components such as seats, toolbox, steering wheel and battery were added. The fuel tank was filled, the battery charged and the engine started – they usuallly fired first time. There were several of these 'assembly lines' in Normandy, at least one under the charge of a former production executive with General Motors, and they were capable of turning out 120 vehicles per day. Most were Jeeps, but some Chevrolet staff cars were also assembled in this way.

Light though it was, the Jeep was felt by some Army personnel to be too heavy for air portability and for manhandling out of difficulty. They therefore called for a lighter vehicle which would weigh around 1000 pounds. The first company to respond was the Crosley Corporation of Cincinnati, Ohio, who had made a light car powered by a 580cc flat-twin Waukesha engine. The same engine went into their Pup, a two seater 4x4 which superficially resembled the Jeep, with a 65-inch wheelbase and weighing 1135 pounds. The Army Ground Forces, Army Air Force and Ordnance ordered 36 Pups for testing. Other lightweights put through their paces in 1943 included a Chevrolet with V-twin Indian motorcycle engine, six Kaisers with 1375cc four-cylinder Continental engines, a Ford with 1162cc four-cylinder engine, two Willys with centrally mounted air-cooled V-twin engines and a stripped Willys MB.

They were all tested up to 10,650 miles over very varied conditions, and testing stopped only when the vehicle broke down and could not be repaired. Only the stripped Willys MB completed the mileage. The mid-engined Willys reached 6627 miles, the Crosleys 3700 and 4700 miles, the Chevrolet 3200 miles and the Kaisers 3380 down to an ignominious 942 miles. For some reason the Ford was not submitted to the full test. None of the 'mini-Jeeps' was adopted for active service as they were unable to cope with the minimal load of 1000 pounds, nor could they fulfil the requirement of carrying a 30mm machine gun. The whole project was cancelled at the end of 1943.

Trucks, up to 1 ton 4x2

Vehicles in this catergory were all modified civilian types, mostly made by Chevrolet, Dodge and Ford. They included vans, pick-up trucks, combined cargo/personnel carriers, with sideways facing seats in the latter case, telephone maintenance trucks and bomb carriers. The latter were made on Ford, GMC and Diamond T chassis, and had open cabs for maximum visibility. They were used for transporting bombs out to aircraft which might be parked more than a mile from their hangars, and

Left: **A Chevrolet 3-ton 6x4 truck with civilian-type front end, which dates it to about 1941, and a Thornton conversion to six-wheel drive.** *(NMM)*

Bottom left: **Three manufacturers supplied 6x4 searchlight carriers during World War Two, Federal, GMC and Mack. This is the GMC version, the AFWX, which carried a Hercules body. Like the other makes, it had a crew cab accomodating five personnel. The trucks were built in 1940 to a French contract, but diverted to Britain after the fall of France in June. By 1941 the British Army had 792, and the US Army took a further 149.** *(NMM)*

were equipped with either manual or power operated lifting cranes. They were used by both Army and Navy Air Forces.

Another popular type in the ½ to 1 ton class was the Suburban, which was really a van with windows and seating inside for six to twelve passengers.

Trucks, up to 1 ton 4x4

This important category was catered for largely by the Dodge Brothers Corporation, a branch of Chrysler Corporation, although a number of other firms had done pioneer work in this class of vehicle. The earliest 4x4s in the ½ ton category were conversions by Marmon-Herrington on a Ford chassis, with station wagon, pick-up or command car bodywork.

Marmon-Herrington Inc. of Indianapolis had been founded in 1931 by Walter C. Marmon, elder brother of Howard who had made the famous Marmon cars, and Colonel Arthur W. Herrington, formerly with the US Army Quartermaster Corps at Fort Holabird. Their first products were large 4x4 and 6x6 trucks and tractors, including the tractors for the Nairn Brothers trans-desert bus service from Damascus to Baghdad. Though they continued to make heavy all-wheel-drive vehicles up to the war, their conversion work on light chassis became much more important. Their first 4x4 Ford

Above: **The famous CCKW, 'Deuce and a half' or 'Jimmy', in its standard form. This is a long wheelbase CCKW-353 with enclosed cab. The engine was a 4.4-litre six-cylinder of 94 bhp, driving through a five-speed gearbox with two-speed transfer box and front-axle declutch. There was also a 6x4 of similar appearance, the CCW-353.**
(Peter Daniels/NMM)

was built in 1936 and they tended to specialise in this make, though they converted a few International pick-ups in 1939.

At the same time General Motors and Dodge were developing their own 4x4 versions of their ½-ton trucks. GMC soon moved on to heavier vehicles, but the Dodge design was taken up by the Army from 1939 onwards, and large numbers were ordered. Dodge were awarded the contract not only because they underbid Ford, but also because of the good record of their 1½-ton 4x4 trucks which had been in Army service since 1935, and because they had the production facility at their new factory at Mound Road, Michigan. Mound Road made practically all of the 400,000 Dodge military vehicles built between 1938 and 1945. The 1939/40 models had similar front end sheet metal to the civilian models and were made with pick-up, seven-passenger suburban, and open command car bodywork. They were powered by the standard 79bhp 3.3-litre six-cylinder engine, with a four-speed gearbox and single-speed transfer box. The equivalent civilian models were rated 1 ton, but in view of the difficult terrain Army vehicles would operate over, they were rated for ½ ton loads. A total of 4,640 of the 1939/40 Series VC were made, of which 844 had closed cabs (pick-up, suburban) and the rest open.

In 1941 the engine was enlarged to 3.8 litres giving 92bhp, and the civilian styling was replaced by a more functional, and cheaper to build, military front end. The new models were designated the Series WC, and were the first World War Two Dodges to see active service. As before, two wheel-

Below:
International's contribution to the 2½-ton 6x6 class was the M-5H6 with larger and more powerful engine than the Stude-baker, at 5.9 litres and 126 bhp. They were used for cargo, refuelling, recovery and tractor work, and some were bodied as fire engines. These two are engaged on road repairs in California in the late 1940s.
(NMM)

bases were offered, 116 or 122 inches, and body types included the command car, radio car, panel van, ambulance, weapons carrier, closed cab pick-up, emergency repair truck and suburban or carryall.

The command car and radio car were very similar in appearance, but the former had a full-length running board on the right-hand side, whereas on the radio car the board was interrupted by the battery box and antenna. On the left-hand side, both models had the running board interrupted by the spare wheel. The panel van and ambulance were externally similar and the carryall used the same sheet metal but had windows in the sides. The weapons carrier was similar to a pick-up with open cab but could carry a .50 Browning M2 machine gun. More than 82,000 of the 1941 Series WC were made, the weapons carrier (34,691) being the most numerous.

All types saw service in all theatres of war in which the US Army was engaged, but by the end of 1943 had mostly been replaced in forward areas by the later ¾-ton Dodge. The ambulances lasted the longest, and some were still in service during the Korean War. One of these 1941-pattern WC ambulances was featured in the television series MASH. The first WCs to see active service were weapons carriers and ambulances supplied to the British Army for use in North Africa.

Extensive testing of the 1941 WC, and possibly feedback from the British Army, revealed to Dodge engineers that, good though the design was, it needed improvement in several ways. Its high build and relatively narrow track made it inclined to tip over, while the tyres were too narrow to cope with deep sand and mud, despite four-wheel drive. These faults were rectified in the 1942-pattern WC which was lower and wider, and became the classic Dodge 4x4 made up to 1945. Although the same engine was used, the load rating was increased to ¾ ton because the wider bodies enabled a greater load to be carried. Tyre size was increased from 7.50x16 to 9x16. Three wheelbases were used in place of the 1941 models' two, but they were shorter, as shown by the following table:-

	1941	1942-5
Weapons Carrier	116"	98"
Command Car	116"	98"
Carryall	116"	114"
Ambulance	122"	121"

In addition to these four body styles there were emergency repair and telephone installation pick-up trucks on the 121-inch wheelbase, and a command field limousine was listed on the 114-inch wheelbase. Despite its appearance in several Dodge manuals, the latter only existed as two prototypes. It differed from the regular Carryall in several

Left: **General Henri Honore Giraud inspects a GMC CCKW at a huge open-air assembly line in North Africa. The truck had been recently delivered to Free French troops.** *(NMM)*

Above: **A Diamond T 975A with open cab towing a generator trailer, passing through Eindhoven in late 1944. The driver is receiving directions from a local Girl Guide.** *(IWM)*

Right: **The first Internationals supplied to the US Army in 1940 were of the newly introduced K line. This is a KR8 tractor on a 137-inch wheelbase, coupled to a Fruehauf 10-ton semi-trailer.** *(NMM)*

Left: **The standard 4-ton 6x6 was made by Diamond T who delivered more than 19,000 for general cargo work as well as wreckers. Standard wheelbases were 151 and 172 inches, but this is a long-wheelbase (201-inch) Model 975A, of which about 1500 were delivered to the Canadian Army. They were fitted with bridging bodies by the Brantford Coach & Body Co of Brantford, Ontario, and used by RCASC bridge companies to transport girders and Bailey bridging equipment, also rafts. The chassis was also used to carry cranes by Bay City and Coles, the latter fitted in England.** *(Public Archives of Canada)*

respects, including four doors at the side, a side-hinged rear door in place of the Carryall's top hinge, and a better equipped interior. It was rejected by the Army as being conspicuous and liable to be strafed by aircraft (a criticism which also applied to the Carryall) and too top-heavy for cross-country operation. The Carryall was dropped in March 1943 for the same reasons, and the Command Car went a year later. Production figures and dates for the ³/₄-ton Dodge are as follows:-

	No. Made	Date
Weapons Carrier	182,655	1942-1945
Command Car	27,166	1942-1944
Carryall	8,400	1942-1943
Ambulance WC54★	26,002	1942-1944
Ambulance WC64★	3,500	1945
Emergency Repair Truck	300	1943-1944
Telephone Installation Truck	607	1943
37mm Gun Carrier	5,380	1942

★Production of the WC54 van-type ambulance was suspended in May 1944 as its body, integral with cab, was too bulky to ship easily and could not be sent CKD. In January 1945 the WC64 was introduced. This had an open cab and a tall, box-shaped body which, although bigger than the WC54, could be easily collapsed for air portability.

Many of the weapons carriers were fitted with a front-mounted winch, which was also featured on the civilian version of the ³/₄-ton Dodge. Known as the Power Wagon, this had a closed cab and 126-inch wheelbase, but was otherwise generally similar to the military models. It was made from 1946 up to 1957, latterly paralleled by the military 4x4 known as the M37.

Dodge was the main supplier of the 4x4 trucks between ½ and 1 ton, but International also made contributions, while Ford built a number of interesting experimental models. The International M-1-4 was similar in size to the Dodge, and used a 3.5-litre 85bhp six-cylinder engine, four-speed gearbox and single-speed transfer box. It was supplied as a weapons carrier and also as an ambulance and was used exclusively by the US Navy and US Marine Corps.

Right: **More than 2700 Autocar U8144T 4x4 tractors were built beween 1941 and 1945. Their four-wheel drive gave them better traction than that of the International 542s, and they were frequently used for carrying bridging equipment semi-trailers. The box behind the cab carries the necessary tools.** *(The Tank Museum, Bovington)*

In 1941 Ford built a Dodge-like command car and pick-up truck powered by their 95bhp 3.9-litre V8 engine, but they were not adopted for production, doubtless because Dodge were meeting the Army's needs. Later in the year they built a series of ³⁄₄-ton cargo trucks that resembled overgrown Jeeps, powered by their new 90bhp six-cylinder engine. One model of these was a 'low-profile' version with the driver seated outside the frame, and another had semi-forward control, with the driver alongside the engine.

Trucks, 1½ to 4 tons 4x2

The majority of Americans trucks made for the civilian market fell into the 1½ to 2 ton category, and considerable numbers of these were used by the Army and Navy, sometimes virtually unmodified, but mostly with protective features such as guards over the radiator grille and headlamps. They were used for a wide variety of duties including personnel transport, radio vans, map making, workshops and aircraft-refuelling tankers. Tippers were widely used for road making and repairing, but few saw such harsh service as those employed on the Burma Road. As the war progressed and supplies of all-wheel-drive trucks came on stream, the 4x2s tended to be used only for domestic duties, as happened in European countries.

Ford supplied 77,604 1½-ton trucks, of which many were assembled at Dagenham and fitted with open cabs for desert work. Chevrolets were also widely used, and their 1½-ton chassis was used by the British Army's LRDG (Long Range Desert Group) for raids deep inside enemy-held territory in the Libyan and Egyptian desert. The 1939 and 1940-type Chevrolets were assembled by General Motors Near East SA at Alexandria, but the 1941-pattern trucks were Canadian-built or imported complete. They all had open cabs and pick-up bodies and carried ample supplies of fuel, oil and water for the trucks, and food and water for the crew.

Other makers who supplied 4x2 trucks included GMC, Diamond T, International, Federal, Mack and White. Most were little modified from their civilian appearance, though for some reason Federal gave their 2½-ton model a military-style front end which gave it the superficial appearance of a 4x4 Chevrolet.

Trucks, 1½ to 4 tons 4x4

As with the smaller four-wheel-drive vehicles, the 1½ ton trucks were made first by Ford using Marmon-Herrington conversion (although they were of typical Ford appearance they carried Marmon-Herrington badges) and Dodge. Several other firms contributed prototypes or small numbers of 4x4s, including Corbitt, Federal, GMC, Reo and Studebaker.

Above: **Two columns of Autocar U8144Ts with the later soft-top cab, towing pontoon bridging equipment, wait to move up to the Rhine at Remagen.** *(The Tank Museum, Bovington)*

Bottom left: **A Mack NM has a new lease of life as a generator truck for Billy Smart's Circus. Registered for civilian use in October 1948, it was photographed at Watford in 1964.** *(Nick Georgano)*

By far the largest number of trucks in this class were made by Chevrolet, whose pilot models were submitted to the Army in 1940. They used the 3.8-litre six-cylinder engine and chassis of the civilian truck, with a four-wheel-drive conversion and military styling common to all bonnetted Chevrolet and GMC trucks. More than 145,000 Chevrolet 1½ tonners were made, compared with 6,532 Internationals and 6,411 Dodges in the same class. As well as general cargo carrying, the Chevrolets were used as signals vans, tippers, earth boring and pole setting units for the rapid erection of telephone lines, and bomb carriers. Some were made in demountable form so that they could be fitted, in three sections, into a Douglas C-47 aircraft. These trucks had open cabs, as did also the bomb carriers, but all other models had closed cabs.

Some forward-control trucks were also converted to four-wheel drive, particularly those of Chevrolet, Ford and GMC. Most of these retained the appearance of their civilian versions, with a high cab. When this was added to the raised chassis necessitated by four-wheel drive the result was a very high centre of gravity. To offset this some low-silhouette trucks were made which had the advantage not only of a low centre of gravity, but also of being less conspicuous on the battlefield. From 1943 to 1944 the Army tested a number of such trucks in different sizes, from ¾ to 3 tons. Designs were submitted by Chevrolet, Ford, International, Corbitt, Reo and Studebaker. Of these only the Ford GTB 1½ ton went into production, with about 6,000 supplied to the US Navy.

The driver sat forward, beside the engine but within the frame, whereas on the Chevrolet proto-

type he sat on an outrigger seat, outside the frame and behind the left front wheel. On the Reo the driver also sat beside the engine, while the 3-ton Corbitt carried its 8.6-litre six-cylinder Hercules RXC engine under a wire mesh cage at the rear. This meant that the truck could be loaded only from the sides, whereas normal practice was, and is, to reverse up to the loading bay, a severe restriction on its practical use.

Studebaker's 1½ ton was a most unusual looking truck, resembling an engineless trailer. On it the driver sat up front, in the centre of the frame, while the 3.8-litre Hercules JXD engine was carried on the right hand side, outside the frame and between the front and rear wheels.

The low-silhouette programme was abandoned at the end of 1944, due to the great cost of putting new designs into production, and the fact that it was impossible to lower the trucks all that much and still preserve reasonable ground clearance and carrying capacity. The pilot models remained at the Aberdeen Proving Grounds in Maryland until the 1950s, when they fell victims to the Korean War scrap-metal drive.

In the 2½- to 4-ton 4x4 class were a number of tractors to be used with semi-trailers. These were made mainly by Autocar and GMC (2½ ton) whilst Autocar, Federal and White manufactured the 4-5 ton. The smaller tractors were derived from civilian models and used civilian-type forward-control cabs, while the heavier tractors used military-style, often open, cabs.

The 2½-ton Autocars were used mainly with fuel tank semi-trailers (some rigid 4x4 tankers were also made by Autocar), while the 81 GMC tractors

Left: **More familiar to British troops than to American was the FWD SU-COE, a 4-ton 4x4 which was provided in large numbers under lend-lease. As well as the GS truck illustrated, the SU-COE was used as an artillery tractor and snowplough.**
(IWM)

Left: **A demobbed AFWX which has aquired a utilitarian single cab and a modified grille. The truck was photographed in the service of the Brussels construction firm, Sogetra, in the 1960s.**
(Arthur Ingram)

supplied in 1940 had the somewhat unusual role of towing horse-box trailers to Cavalry assembly areas, often over poor roads or across country. The 4-5 ton tractors all had short nose, semi-forward control bonnets with closed cabs on the 1941 models, and open cabs from 1942 to 1945.

The Autocar U-7144-T was powered by a 112bhp six-cylinder Hercules RXC engine of 8.6-litre capacity, and had a five-speed gearbox with two-speed transfer box. White produced an identical model, and the design was also made by Kenworth and Marmon-Herrington later in the war. The Federal 94x43 was generally similar, with the same engine, but had a rounded grille instead of the Autocar's flat grille. Some of the open-cabbed

Federals had a .50 Browning M2 machine gun above the cab, to defend convoys when passing through hostile territory. They often pulled food-carrying trailers, including refrigerated vans, and also bridging equipment.

The best known rigid 4x4 truck in the 3-4 ton category was the FWD Model HAR, made by the Four-Wheel Drive Auto Company of Clintonville, Wisconsin. Modified civilian, and military, models were made, all powered by a 5.2-litre six-cylinder Waukesha 6 BZ engine developing 88bhp. They had five-speed constant-mesh gearboxes with single-speed chain-driven transfer boxes which gave permanently engaged four-wheel drive. The civilian model was known as the HAR-01 and

Above: **A Mack NO towing a 155mm gun. Above the open cab is a machine gun; every fourth NO made was fitted with an M36 ring mount to take a .30 or .50 calibre machine gun. Contrasted with the Mack is a Jeep towing an anti-tank gun.**
(Fred Crismon Collection)

could be identified by its closed cab and rounded radiator grille. The first order for these came from the Canadian Government who bought the chassis from Clintonville and shipped them to FWD's Canadian plant at Kitchener, Ontario, where they were fitted with bodies made by Brentford Coach and Body Ltd. Most of them had ordinary GS bodies but there was an articulated version with trailers by either Fruehauf or Frost & Wood. This was known as the HAR-03, and was rated for a 6 ton load, compared with 3 to 4 tons for the HAR-01. Like the latter, the 03 was ordered exclusively by the Canadians, though a number of both types came to Britain via Canada. Some 01s were used with four-wheeled drawbar trailers for transporting radar equipment.

In 1943 the US Army placed an order for the HAR, which was supplied in militarised form with a flat radiator grille, squared-off mudguards and an open cab with canvas top. This was known as the HAR-1, and although between 7,000 and 9,000 were produced for the US Army, it seems that most of them were supplied via Lend-Lease to other countries. This was because the FWD could not be fitted into the standardised truck design, so there was little inter-changeability of parts. The Waukesha engine, although a popular unit for commercial trucks, was not used by any other make of army truck. Some were assembled by General

Motors Holdens, Australian plant at Pagewood, New South Wales.

Among the tasks of HAR-1s used by the British Army was to tow four-wheeled smoke-generating trailers, which provided cover for attacking troops. The RAF used HAR-1s as snowploughs, as they also did the forward control FWD SU-COE (see page 157). The trucks were also used, during and after the war, by the armies of France, the Netherlands, Iran and China.

Trucks, 1½ to 4 tons, 6x4 & 6x6

The 6x6 was an obvious extension of the 4x4 layout when a larger wheelbase was needed. Most civilian six-wheeled trucks drove on only one, or at most, two axles, but military needs dictated maximum traction over poor surfaces, and by the mid-1930s several American manufacturers had built trucks in this class, in sizes varying from 2½ to 7 tons capacity. The standardised QMC fleet included 6x6s from 2½ tons up and when the Quartermaster Corps were forbidden to continue making trucks, the way was open for commercial manufacturers to bid for this market. Colonel Arthur Herrington had been responsible for America's first 6x6, a modified Liberty truck of 1924, and when he set up

the Marmon-Herrington company one of his first products was a 2½-ton 6x6, joined over the next few years by 3-ton and 6-ton models.

Most of the other firms who made 6x6s in the 1930s were the smaller businesses who could adapt more easily to specialised needs, as their trucks were all hand assembled. They included Biederman, Clydesdale, Corbitt, Hug and Indiana, though later entrants into this field included Studebaker and, most importantly, GMC.

1½ tons

Before discussing the famous 2½-ton GMC, there was a smaller 6x6 made in considerable numbers. This was the 1½-ton Dodge Model T223 made from 1943 to 45, a lengthened version of the ¾-ton WC with a tandem axle at the rear, and overall length of 215 ins compared with the WC's 165 ins. It offered about 40% greater cargo space than the four-wheeler, though the engine was exactly the same; despite the use of a two-speed transfer box this limited its suitability for carrying a full load over rough country. Most were used as 12-passenger personnel carriers, though some were tested as rocket launchers, carrying four 12 foot rocket tubes firing forwards over the cab. To protect the crew

from the back blast of the rockets, a crude steel cab was provided, unlike the regular T223s which had open cabs. Rockets had not achieved a very high standard of accuracy during World War Two, and were only used when a massive barrage attack was required. It is not known whether the Dodge Rocket Launcher, any more than the equivalent Jeep, was used in active service, although the Soviet Army certainly used similarly equipped 6x6 Studebakers, which fired their weapons sideways. A total of 43,224 Dodge T223s were made; they remained in US Army service until the early 1950s, and were used by other nations including France, Greece, Turkey, Israel and several Latin American countries until considerably later.

The other company to build 1½-ton 6x6 trucks was International Harvester. Their M-3-6 was an extended version of the 4x4 M-2-4 ¾ ton and used the same engine. It was made in much smaller numbers than the Dodge, and was supplied only to the Marine Corps.

2½ tons

By far the most important 6x6 truck in the US Army, and the vehicle made in larger numbers than any other, including the Jeep, was the 2½-ton

Above: **The biggest Mack cargo truck of World War Two was the NO, a 6x6 for 7½ ton loads. It was powered by a Mack EY six-cylinder petrol engine of 11,585cc and 157bhp. Transmission was by a five-speed gearbox with two speed transfer. 2050 NOs were built between 1943 and 1945.** *(Fred Crismon Collection)*

Right: **A Corbitt
50SD6 of the US
Army Engineers
towing a low-
loading trailer
passing through
the ruins of
Mönchengladbach.
Behind it is a GMC
CCKW-353
followed by
another Corbitt.**
*(The Tank Museum,
Bovington)*

GMC, nicknamed the 'Deuce and a half' or
'Jimmy'. The first such trucks made by General
Motors were delivered to the US Army in 1939.
They had civilian-type grilles, bonnets and cabs,
though the liberally chromed grille was protected
by a heavy guard. The engine was a regular commercial GM unit, an ohv six-cylinder engine of
4.4-litres, developing 104bhp. Transmission was by
a four-speed gearbox with two-speed transfer box
and optional drive to the front axle. The initial
model of 1939 was known as the ACKWX-353,
according to the following code:-

A =	1939
C =	conventional cab
K =	front wheel drive
W =	tandem rear drive
X =	non-standard wheelbase, i.e., different from any civilian model
353 =	164 inch wheelbase (the alternative 145inch wheelbase was coded 352)

This nomenclature was followed through all the
wartime GMCs, though the X suffix was dropped
except, for some reason, for the forward control
models. The ACKWX-353 was an extended version
of the ACK 353 1½ ton, of which the French Army
ordered 2,000. They also ordered the six-wheeler
in considerable numbers, but France fell to the
Germans before many were delivered, so they were
re-directed to Britain in the latter part of 1940,
contributing to the enormous dollar debt which
eventually led to the establishment of Lend-Lease.
The forward-control version on the shorter wheelbase was the AFKWX-352; at first a civilian grille
and cab were used, but from 1944 onwards open
cabs were featured. Although the AFKWX was
made, on both wheelbases, from 1940 to 45, only
7,232 were built, compared with more than
500,000 normal control models from GMC alone,
with a further 300,000 being contributed by
International, Reo and Studebaker.

In 1941 the militarised version of the normal control 6x6 went into production, code named CCKW-
352 or 353. The initial letter indicated the year of
design, not production, though the 1940 models were
similar to the 1939 there was never a BCKW. No basic
changes were made to the 1941 design, so the code
CCKW was used for all subsequent trucks made up to
the end of the war. Apart from the militarized front
end and cab the CCKW did not differ greatly from
the ACKWX, and it is interesting that such a successful design should have used such a high proportion of
off-the-shelf civilian parts.

As the American military vehicle historian
Major Fred Crismon said, "It makes one wonder
why the armed forces for so many years insisted on
developing military trucks, from the ground up, as
totally exclusive military designs, at nearly double

Above: **This is a White 6x6, differing from the Corbitt in having a 25,000 pounds capacity winch ahead of the radiator, though this could be fitted to either make. The canvas top of the body and trailer concealed two 2000-gallon fuel tanks.**
(Fred Crismon Collection)

the cost of commercially based models. None will probably ever serve any better than these machines did, and these were simple."

An important difference between the ACKWX and the CCKW was that the latter had a five-speed gearbox in addition to the two-speed transfer box, giving ten forward speeds from crawling up to 50mph. On the 6x4 version, known as the CCW, the low-speed range in the transfer box was blocked out, as this truck was not expected to operate in severe off-road conditions. Not that on-road conditions were very good after they had been pounded by thousands of trucks and tracked vehicles. Far fewer 6x4s were made than 6x6, and were rated for 2½ to 5 ton loads. Federal, International and Mack, also GMC were the manufacturers.

At the same time as GMC was developing the CCKW, other manufacturers were following US Government directives and developing their own trucks in this class. International built their M5-6 prototype in December 1941; it was generally similar to the GMC, but used its maker's own 111bhp six-cylinder engine. Long and short wheelbases and steel or canvas cabs were offered. Most International 6x6s, like their smaller models, went to the US Navy or Marine Corps. The Studebaker US-6 had a 87bhp Hercules JXD engine and, like its contemporaries, came with open or closed cabs and a wide variety of bodywork. The Reo U3 was

almost identical to the Studebaker as production was subcontracted (after the war the situation was reversed with Studebaker making Reo's 2½-ton 6x6 truck, the 'Eager Beaver'), whereas International and Studebaker produced their own designs, although in the interests of standardisation they were generally similar to the GMC. As well as their use by US forces, these 6x6 trucks were supplied in large numbers to other countries via Lend-Lease. A high proportion of the Studebakers went to Russia via Iran; they remained in service with the Soviet Army for some time after the war, and later GAZ truck engines were based on the Hercules. Production figures for the 2½-ton 6x6, some approximate, are as follows:-

GMC =	562,750
Studebaker =	197,000 +
International =	37,088
Reo =	22,204

Up to 1942 the bodies of the CCKW were made of steel, but a severe shortage of this metal led the army to look for other materials, of which the logical one was wood. From mid-1942 CCKW and many other Army trucks were fitted with wooden bodies, built by a large number of companies organised by the Ordnance Industry Integration Committee for Wood Cargo Bodies. A variety of hardwoods

Left: **The WC54 was the most popular ambulance on the Dodge T214 chassis; 26,000 were made between 1942 and 1944. They could accommodate four stretcher cases or seven sitting patients.**
(J Spencer-Smith)

Below: **The WC64 was known as the 'Ambulance, Collapsible, $^3/_4$ ton 4x4'. It was designed so that the body sides and top could be dropped down into the lower part of the body, together with the cab and windscreen. This made it easily transportable by air. Introduced in January 1945, 3500 were made.**
(The Tank Museum, Bovington)

Right and below:
A standard model Jeep, restored by George Alexander of the Military Vehicle Conservation Group (Dorset).
(J Spencer-Smith)

Left: **The armour on this Jeep is a field modification. The lettering on the bumper indicates that it was used by the 82nd Airborne division, Company A, vehicle number 2.**
(Vehicle displayed at the Victory Memorial Museum)

Below: **A Jeep transformed into an ambulance, with two stretchers over the bonnet and two at the rear. It was operated by 633 Medical Battalion, First Army.**
(Vehicle displayed at the Victory Memorial Museum)

Right: **A multiple gun carrier with quadruple turret-type .50 machine guns. These were built by White as the M16 and by International as the M17. The M13 and M14 were similar but had only two machine guns. Even in their lighter personnel carrier form, these halftracks weighed 8½ tons, a lot for the 147bhp engine to pull.**
(John Blackman)

Below: **The White M3A1 Scout Car in its 1939 form, which was made throughout the war. Note the front-mounted roller to prevent the car from embedding itself in soft ground. Most had Hercules engines, but some were fitted with slightly smaller Budas to improve fuel consumption.**
(J Spencer-Smith)

Left: **The Dodge 214 command reconaissance car was the third generation of such vehicles, with more powerful engine and better cross-country abilities than its predecessors, thanks to a wider track and bigger tyres. This is the WC56; when fitted with a frontal winch it became the WC57.**
(J Spencer-Smith)

Centre left: **A Dodge T214 in GS form when it was known as the WC52. This model was sometimes nicknamed the Beep.**
(Vehicle displayed at the Victory Memorial Museum)

Below: **The T223/WC63 was the 6x6 version of the Dodge 214, and was rated for 1$\frac{1}{2}$ ton loads. Without a winch, which added 450 pounds to the net weight, it was the WC62. Mechanical components were basically the same as those in the 214. In addition to the weapons carrier illustrated, the T223 could be fitted with one or two .50 machine guns or a multiple rocket launcher. They were widely used after the war by the armies of France, Switzerland, Greece, Turkey, Israel and Portugal, and by the Swedish Air Force when they had locally made van bodies.**
(The Tank Museum, Bovington)

Above: **A GMC CCKW-353 with canvas-topped cab and cut-away doors.**
(*J Spencer-Smith*)

Centre:
Studebaker's version of the GMC 6x6 truck. Despite a similiar appearance, the Studebakers had no mechanical components in common with the GMC apart from small items such as light bulbs. The Hercules engine was so durable that its design was copied by the Russians for their GAZ trucks, which used GMC-pattern engines until quite recently.
(*John Blackman*)

Right: **This GMC CCKW-353 is equipped with a Le Roi Model D318 air-compressor.**
(*Vehicle displayed at the Victory Memorial Museum*)

Left and centre: **Diamond T's contribution to the heavy wrecker was the model 969, a 6x6 chassis powered by an 8.7-litre side-valve Hercules engine. The two cable-operated booms had a capacity of five tons each. They could be used either together at the rear, or one on each side, with one acting as the stabilising element while the other lifted the load.**
(The Tank Museum, Bovington)

Below: **A well-restored M1A1 heavy wrecker of the standard design made by Kenworth and Ward La France. It had an 8.2-litre 145bhp six-cylinder Continental engine.**
(The Tank Museum, Bovington)

Right: **The International H-542 4x2 tractor, normally seen with a 10-ton semi-trailer, was one of the mainstays of long-distance routes across France, such as the Red Ball Express. Some were also made by Marmon-Herrington and Kenworth.**
(The Tank Museum, Bovington)

Below: **Pick-up version of the Dodge ½-ton 4x4. The front end is militarised but the cab is still the civilian model. Later models had open cabs and wider track and were rated as ¾ tonners.**
(The Tank Museum, Bovington)

Left: **This Mack NO was still used by the Geneva-based hauliers Naturel Le Coultre in 1967.** (Nick Georgano)

Below centre: **Many FWD SU-COEs found their way into civilian use after the war. They were particularly popular with fairground showmen, but this one is a timber tractor, seen passing through Brecon in 1958.** (Arthur Ingram)

were used, treated for protection against rot and termites. Obviously some parts remained of steel construction, such as the bonnet and wings, but the weight of the steel in a CCKW was reduced from 1700 to 700 pounds.

The uses to which the 6x6 trucks were put were many. Their main job was as a general load or personnel carrier, and one of the most famous, the 'Red Ball Express' (presumably named after a well-known American trucking company, Red Ball Transit of Indianapolis, who made their own trucks for a few years in the 1920s), operated across Northern France between August and November 1944. The rapid advance of the allied armoured divisions meant that lines of communication between the front and the huge supply depots in Normandy lengthened daily, and the supply needs, not only of the advancing armies but also of the liberated civilian population, were enormous. Paris alone required a daily minimum of 2,400 tons of supplies. The railways were largely out of action, so the US Army organised a massive 'road lift' which involved more than 5,400 trucks, most of them 6x4 or 6x6 GMCs. The mileage of the official routes of the 'Red Ball Express' was more than 690 miles, and a daily average of 5,143 tons was delivered. The largest daily tonnage was 12,540 tons, achieved on 29 August. Other supplies were organised over dif-

Bottom: **C.1941 Ward La France M1 6x6 heavy wrecker with Gar Wood swinging boom crane and front-mounted winch. About 1500 of this design were made by Ward La France and 530 by Kenworth.** (Bart Vanderveen Collection)

ferent routes, called the 'White Ball Express', while the British Second Army was supplied by the 'Red Lion Express'. Once the port of Antwerp had fallen to the Allies, the need for these long-distance supply routes disappeared, though of course convoys of trucks continued to provide supplies for the troops serving at the front.

Among the many other uses to which the CCKW and its relatives were put were the following:-

Dump Truck for road making : about 800 built
Transportation of bridge-building equipment
Air Compressor by Le Roi for construction
equipment, pneumatic drills or inflation of rubber boats
Breakdown Equipment
Petrol Tankers : 660 or 750 gallons,
made by Heil Company
Water Tankers : 700 gallons
Water Purification
Field Operating Theatres, Dental surgeries
and First Aid posts
Mobile Canteens (Clubmobiles)
Mobile Cinemas (Cinemobiles) mostly driven
by girls of the American Red Cross.
Mobile Command Posts
Mobile Workshops
Bomb Transporters
High-Lift Vans for loading large aircraft
Rocket Launchers : used by the Russian Army on
the Studebaker chassis, nicknamed 'Stalin's Organs.'

The 6x6 was also the basis for the amphibious DUKW described on page 169.

An air-portable version of the CCKW was developed in 1944, and more than 7,250 were made, though there is no record of having been used in strategic airlifts. After the war they remained on the strengths of European armies in France, the Netherlands, Denmark and Norway.

The CCKW remained in US Army service until 1956, when it was superseded by the new generation of 6x6 2½ tonner, the M series built by Reo, Studebaker and later by Kaiser-Jeep and AM General. Thus it went all through the Korean War, where it found itself on the opposite side to some of its brothers which had passed from the Russians to the North Koreans. The French Army received large numbers of CCKWs after the war, some of which were still in service at the end of the 1970s. Others, at least 300, were transferred from France to Israel in October 1956, and took part in the war against Egypt. As recently as May 1984 the French disposed of 300 open-cabbed CCKW-353s.

Ex-army 6x6s played an important part in European recovery in the early post-war years, when new trucks were in very short supply. As well as general load carriers, they were used on building sites, as breakdown trucks, tankers, fire engines and a few as buses. In France, several hundred fire

engines were built on reconditioned CCKW chassis by Louis Froger and then Landreau. They were first sold in 1952, and the Landreau versions were still available in the mid-1980s.

4 tons

The next category in which 6x6s were supplied to the US Army was the 4-ton truck. These had been made in small numbers before the war by Biederman, Indiana, Autocar, Diamond T and White. The contract for large-scale production went to Diamond T, and figures for the other makers were twenty Biedermans, eight Autocars, eighty Whites and an unknown number of Indianas, probably not more than twenty. Reo also submitted a prototype.

The Diamond T was a powerful bonnetted truck which could also do duty as a tractive unit, and indeed it was more famous during and after the war as a heavy wrecker. The engine was a six-cylinder 8.6-litre Hercules RXC which developed 131bhp. It had a five-speed gearbox with two-speed transfer box. Most were delivered with front-mounted winch. The basic model was the 967, while later cargo carriers were the 968 and 968A. Models 969A and B were wreckers, 970A a pontoon carrier and 972 a dump truck. Two wheelbases were available, 151 inches and 172 inches. The 4-ton Diamond T had a top speed limited by a governor to 40mph, and an average fuel consumption of 3mpg. Apart from the duties already mentioned they were also used as map reproduction equipment vans and machinery carriers for metal turning, screw cutting, etc, on a heavy-duty lathe (Canadian Army Model 975). One of these 975 chassis was the basis for the Command Caravan used by General Henry Crerar, commander of the First Canadian Army, from October 1944 to the end of the war. Some were fitted with cranes made by either Bay City or Coles. Total production of the 4-ton Diamond T was 19,168, made up of the following types:-

Cargo or Pontoon bodies	10,551
Wreckers	6,420
Chassis for special equipment	2,197
	19,168

The only other truck in the 4-ton 6x6 class was the so-called 'Jumbo Jeep' built by the Canadian-American Truck Co. This had a very long wheelbase of 200 inches and was to have been powered by one of three interchangeable engines, the Continental 22R, the Hercules RXC or the Waukesha 6 SRKR. Only one was made (together with a 4-5 ton 4x4) and it proved unsatisfactory in its cooling arrangements and also broke an axle

during drawbar tests. It did not appear until 1943, by which time the Diamond T was well established, so it is hardly surprising that a new design from an unknown company was not ordered.

Heavy Trucks, 4x2, 4x4, 6x4, 6x6

Most trucks for loads of 5 tons and up were six-wheelers, but there were a few 4x2 and 4x4 vehicles in the 5 ton class. The US Army and Navy used Autocar, Diamond T, Federal, GMC, International and Mack 4x2s in modified civilian form, and also the military-pattern International H-542-9 4x2 tractor. This was originally rated for a 5-ton semi-trailer, but with heavier springs it could easily haul a 10 ton load, and the improved H-542-11 made from 1943 onwards was always considered a 10 tonner. It had a snub-nosed short bonnet and open

cab and was powered by a 7.4-litre 143bhp six-cylinder International Red Diamond engine. They were mainly used on long distance supply routes such as the 'Red Ball Express' in Europe or the Burma Road. Production of the H-542-9 (M425 in Army numbering) was 4,640 and of the H-542-11 (M426) 10,978. The latter design was subcontracted to Marmon-Herrington who made 3,200 and Kenworth who made 1,100. They survived in civilian haulage for many years after the war, and in France more than 500 trucks have been made, based on the M426. These were the work of a tanker operator, Antoine Lohéac, who began with slightly modified ex-army tractors in the 1950s, and gradually included more and more components currently available, such as engines by Berliet or DAF, and fibreglass cabs made at Lohéac's premises near Rouen. No Lohéac has ever been scrapped: they are rebuilt as components wear out, and the frames of current Lohéacs are still the old World War Two units, as are the steering wheels. Although the cabs are closed and thoroughly modern, the snub-nosed Lohéac tractors of the 1980s bear a family resemblance to their American ancestors made forty years earlier.

Most 4x4 trucks in the 5-6 ton category were made by Autocar, FWD and Mack. The Autocar U8144 was similar to the 4-ton U7144 already described and, like the latter, was made in truck and tractor form with open or closed cabs. FWD made several trucks in this class, all with forward control. The SU-COE became very familiar to British troops as they were mainly produced for Lend-Lease, and were used as general cargo trucks, artillery tractors and snowploughs. They were powered by an 8.3-litre SRKR Waukesha 126bhp engine and four- or five-speed gearboxes with single-speed transfer boxes and permanently engaged four-wheel drive. After the war they became popular with fairground operators. Few SU-COEs went to the American forces, although the Marine Corps used a few short-wheelbase models with open cabs as tractors for quick boarding on landing craft. These had a larger Waukesha engine of 9.3-litres. FWD also made the YU 6 ton which was used for transporting and erecting pontoon bridges. By the use of a box-type boom the pontoon sections could be lifted from the truck bed and placed in position.

Mack's contribution to the 4x4 class was the NJU, a forward-control truck/tractor derived from the maker's civilian CH and CJ models. Used for pulling pontoon trailers among other duties, the NJU was powered by a Mack-built 8.7-litre six-cylinder engine and had a five-speed gearbox with two-speed transfer box. Essentially a conversion design, it was made from 1940 to 1941 only, after which the Autocar and FWD models took over. Total production of the NJU was 692.

Left: **Reo's 6x6 was used as a recovery vehicle, fire engine and prime mover for a 4000-gallon semi-trailer tanker. It was powered by a 14-litre Hercules HMD engine. This one was operated in Britain by the US Army Air Force.** *(Nick Baldwin Collection)*

Bottom left: **This view of the White 6x6 shows it without its cargo truck disguise. The Heil tank bodies were divided into tanks of 490, 500, 498 and 512 gallons. Earlier models had closed cabs.** *(Fred Crismon Collection)*

The heaviest trucks in the US Army without driven front axles were the 8-10 ton 6x4s made chiefly by Mack but also by Autocar, Corbitt, Federal, International and White. The Mack EXBX was developed in 1939 from the civilian BX model, in response to a French contract for a tank transporter. After the fall of France the balance of the order was transferred to the British Army who used them in North Africa. They were powered by 8.5-litre 136bhp Mack-Lanova diesel engines, the first American military trucks to use diesel fuel. Because of the ready availability of cheap petrol, American truck makers were very slow to take to diesel compared with their European counterparts, and very few civilian or military trucks were diesel-powered at the time of World War Two. In 1940 the basically civilian EXBX gave way to the NR series which was made with open or closed cab and used for general hauling as well as tank transportation. The 6x4 rigid truck was suitable only for relatively small tanks, and later in the war larger tractor/trailer units by Diamond T and Pacific were normally used for this work. One of the mainstays of the 'Red Ball Express' and other long-distance delivery routes, the NR was made in various models from 1940 to 1944. Production totalled 15,528, compared with 260 of the EXBX.

The International 10-ton 6x4 was known to the makers as the H-542-9 Modified and to the Army as the T48. This had the front end and open cab of the H542 4x2 tractor, and the rear bogie from a 4-ton 6x6 Diamond T. Not many were made, and they were used mainly on the 'Ting Hao Overland Express' running from India through Burma to China, a 1,100-mile run over very difficult roads.

The White 1064 was another diesel-powered truck, using an 11-litre Cummins HB600 six-cylinder engine developing 137bhp. It had a military-style front end and cab shared with the 6-ton 6x6 made by White, Corbitt, Brockway, FWD and Ward La France. A total of 2,500 White 1064s were made. Other 6x4s made in smaller numbers were the Federal 604 fuel tanker based on their 20-ton tank transporter (see page 165), and the Corbitt 40SD6 which was a tractor for long distance highway work and was very unusual among military vehicles in featuring a sleeper cab. Actually this Corbitt, although operated by the Army, was not strictly a military design and was not used outside the United States. The 6-ton 6x6 trucks were mostly made to an identical design, built at first by Corbitt and White, and as demand increased by Brockway, FWD and Ward La France. Corbitt built the pilot models, between 1939 and 1941, powered

Below: **A Mack LMSW 6x4 heavy wrecker with body equipment by Gar Wood. This included an oxy-acetylene welding and cutting gear. It is emerging from a landing craft, probably on the Normandy beachhead in 1944.** *(Public Archives of Canada)*

Above: **A Ward La France operated by Sogetra and seen near Brussels in 1971. The squared mudguards identify it as an M1A1, the closed cab having been fitted after the war.**

(Arthur Ingram)

by a 12.7-litre Hercules HXC six-cylinder engine. A 25,000 pound winch driven from the transfer box was mounted amidships, behind the cab, and the general layout was similar to smaller 6x6 trucks.

Towards the end of 1941 production began of a modified design with larger Hercules engine, the 202 bhp HXD which displaced a massive 14 litres. A more military-style front end was featured, and from mid-1942 open cab versions were made. The first production models carried Corbitt or White nameplates on the front of the bonnet, but this practice was soon dropped, and the two makes could only be identified by their date plates or by small differences such as that the White was slightly lower geared, and three inches longer, while the Corbitt was 535 pounds heavier, at 22,070 pounds, and had a higher axle weight rating. The standard wheelbase was 185 inches, but crane carriers and fire engines were made on a 197-inch wheelbase, while that of the pontoon bridge carrier ran to 220 inches. Other variants included a 2000 gallon fuel tanker, power generating van and tractor. The latter was the main task of the 666, either for artillery or general cargo. Some fuel tankers towed a four-wheeled tanker trailer. They were often disguised as ordinary cargo trucks, with canvas tilt tops, to make them less vulnerable to air attack. A few 666s were equipped as snowploughs, with three banks of rotary blades driven by a separate engine carried behind the cab, where the winch was normally located. Incidentally the winch had a 25,000 pound

capacity on the White 666, but only 15,000 pounds on the production Corbitt 50SD6, although the pilot model Corbitt winches were also rated at 25,000 pounds capacity.

The only 6 ton which did not conform to the standardised type was the Mack NM series. Introduced in 1939 these had 11.6-litre six-cylinder Mack EY engines, and five-speed gearboxes with two-speed transfer boxes. Like the standardised trucks they had a winch mounted behind the cab, a 25,000 pound Gar Wood US4S. The Wisconsin transfer box and Timken axles were identical to those on the Corbitt/White models. Between 1940 and 1945 the NM was made in seven different models (the last was NM8, as NM4 was omitted from the numbering) which differed in small ways. Mack followed other makers in adopting the open cab in 1942 on the NM5, although the final NM8 reverted to a closed cab. Total production of the NM was 7,236.

The 7½-ton Mack NO used the same engine as the NM, but had a shorter wheelbase (156 compared with 177 inches) and a greater ground clearance. This was because it had double reduction gears in the steering ends of the front axle, so that the axle housing and differential were higher than the wheel hubs, ground clearance was 14 inches and overall height 10ft 4ins. The NO was also distinguished by its massive 40,000 pound winch mounted in front, ahead of the radiator. Its main purpose was an Artillery Tractor, pulling the 15-ton

Left: **The trailers loaded by the Diamond T 969s were as often as not pulled by Diamond T 980s. These were larger trucks, whose ohv Hercules DXFE diesel engines displaced 14.6 litres. The standard trailer for use with the 980 was the three-axle twelve-wheel M9 for a 45-ton load. This one is carrying a Sherman tank.** *(The Tank Museum, Bovington)*

Long Tom field gun, though it could also carry a 7½ ton load, or a 5 ton load while pulling the gun. Longer wheelbase versions of the NO4 and NO5 were used as heavy wreckers.

The other 7½-ton 6x6s were built to a standard Army Air Force specification by Biederman, Federal and Reo. They all had big six-cylinder Hercules engines, either the 12.7-litre HXC or the 14-litre HMD, and were mostly built as wreckers or tractors for fuel tanker or aircraft recovery semi-trailers. The overall length of the latter could be as great as 65ft 9ins. A feature of these trucks and tractors was the use of Cleveland Pneumatic air-springs to supplement the ordinary front springs, these cylinders being a ready identifying feature. Unlike most military trucks these were never made with open cabs, probably because they were seldom engaged in front line duties.

Heavy Wreckers

The Wrecker, or Breakdown Lorry as it was called in Britain, had been around for a long time for the recovery of stranded or crashed cars, but little attention had been given to similar work for heavy

trucks. With the approach of war it became obvious that disabled trucks would have to be retrieved quickly and efficiently, and the Army set about ordering suitable vehicles. As always Colonel Herrington was ready to supply military needs, and as early as 1935 had built a swinging boom crane on one of his Marmon-Herrington 6x6 chassis. Two years later this class of vehicle was officially recognised as a 'Truck, Wrecking, Heavy, M1.' Its role was to recover from ditches or other awkward spots and tow every type of Army vehicle currently in service, tracked as well as wheeled, and also to effect repairs in the field. The first company to supply wreckers to this specification was Corbitt, who used their 6x6 chassis powered by a 12.7-litre Hercules HXC engine. Few of these were made, and the first quantity deliveries of wreckers came from two small companies at opposite ends of the continent, Ward La France of Elmira, NY, and Kenworth of Seattle, Washington.

In 1939 Ward La France had built a very small number of 6x6 chassis, six of which they equipped with Holmes twin-boom cranes. It was possibly this which encouraged the Ordnance Department to look to Elmira when they wanted to order wreckers in quantity. It is an advantage of a small

Bottom left: **The later version of the Ward La France/Kenworth heavy wrecker, the M1-A1. Made from 1943, it could be easily distinguished by its open cab and mounting for a .50 machine gun. Behind it is a Kenworth M1 with closed cab.** *(Bart Vanderveen Collection)*

firm that it can turn to specialised work quickly, and Ward La France had made a point of tailoring their vehicles to customers' needs. In fact, so specialised were they that the initial order for 69 heavy wreckers may well have been the largest single order they had received in their 22-year history. On the West Coast the San Francisco Ordnance Department ordered 300 wreckers of similar design from Kenworth, a company known worldwide today for heavy trucks but then largely of local fame. It was unusual to see a Kenworth east of the Rockies until after the war.

The two M1 designs were basically similar, both using an 8.2-litre six-cylinder ohv Continental 22R engine which developed 145bhp. They had five-speed Fuller gearboxes and two-speed Timken transfer boxes, with optional drive to the front axle. The crane was made by Gar Wood of Detroit, and was initially turned manually, although of course the actual lifting was carried out by an engine-driven winch. From 1943 onwards the crane was fully power operated. As well as the crane winch, the M1s carried a front-mounted 20,000 pound Gar Wood winch. The main external differences between the two makes lay in the radiator and bonnet shape, flat-topped on the Kenworth and slightly pointed on the Ward La France, and the mudguards which were semi-circular on the Kenworth and straight at the rear on the Ward La France. Internally the main difference was that the Kenworth had rod and lever linkage for the transfer

box and front winch, while the Ward La France had cable linkage.

In 1943 a more thoroughly standardised design appeared, later to be officially known as the M1A1. This had an open cab above which was a ring-mount for a .50 machine gun (found on many, but not all, M1A1s) and squared mudguards. Engine and transmission were as on the earlier M1. This standard design was made up to the end of the war, and remained in US Army service up to the mid - 1950s. 'Demobbed' examples served as heavy wreckers in Europe and the USA for many years, and a number which became surplus to American requirements passed to the French and Swiss Armies.

Although the initial order to Kenworth was much larger than that given to Ward La France, in the long run the latter made the majority of both types. Actual figures are as follows:-

	Ward La France	Kenworth
M1	c1,500	530
M1A1	c3,425	310
Total	4,925	840

Most other heavy wreckers used by the American forces were based on 6x6 chassis already described. These included the Diamond T 969 of which 6,420 carried Holmes equipment, and the standardised design made by Biederman, Federal and Reo. These were used by the Army and Navy Air Forces, and their main task was to lift disabled

Below: **A Pacific M26 6x6 tank recovery tractor with armoured cab, and coupled to an M15 trailer carrying a Chrysler-built T92 240mm Howitzer motor carriage. This weighed nearly 57 tons, well above the 44 ton load for which the Pacific was rated. Gross weight was 91.78 tons, and maximum speed 28mph.**
(Fred Crismon Collection)

aircraft on to trailers pulled by tractor versions of the same chassis. It was claimed that one wrecker could "pick up a medium bomber with ease" and that two of them working together could "swing the heaviest war plane now in production without a quiver or groan."

The Biederman C2 chassis used a Silent Hoist crane, while Federals and Reos both had Gar Wood equipment. Both cranes had a capacity of 10 tons. Wrecking equipment was also made on the Mack NO chassis, but only two were built, the NO4 supplied to the Air Corps and the NO5 for the Artillery. Other chassis to carry heavy wrecking equipment included Autocar 4x2 and 4x4, and Sterling 6x4 and 6x6.

Tank Recovery Transporters

During the 1930s little attention had been paid to specialised tank transporters, because most tanks were small enough to be carried on a long-wheel-base 6x4 truck such as the Mack EXBX. The demand for a more powerful and larger unit came from Britain, where the standard Scammell 30-ton transporter (see page 49) was too small for the new Churchill tanks, and anyway could not be produced in sufficiently large numbers. In 1940 a British purchasing commission began discussions with the US Quartermaster Corps, and the Diamond T Motor Company of Chicago was

approached to build a 6x4 tractor capable of pulling a load up to 45 tons on a three-axle low-loading trailer. For a power unit they chose a 14.6-litre six cylinder Hercules DXFE diesel engine, one of the few diesels used by the US Army during the war. The Fuller gearbox gave four speeds, and a three-speed transfer box, also by Fuller, gave a total of twelve forward speeds. Diamond T was an assembled truck, and most components were bought in, including Timken axles, Ross steering, Westinghouse air brakes, etc., though the chassis frame and body panels were made by Diamond T. Mounted behind the cab was a 20-ton winch. The trailer was a three-axle type with four dual wheels on each axle, made by Rogers Brothers Corporation of Albion, Pennsylvania, and later subcontracted to Fruehauf and other manufacturers. The Rogers trailer had a capacity of 45 tons, and there was also a 40-ton British trailer, made by Crane, Dyson and others. In addition to these full trailers, designed for recovering 38½-ton Churchill tanks, there was a two-axle semi-trailer made by Shelvoke & Drewry with a 30 ton capacity. In service the Rogers design proved unsatisfactory for loads much above 30 tons, with frequent tyre blowouts and sheared wheel studs. In North Africa and Italy crews did not normally stop for one blowout, they waited for two or three, which were not slow in coming, in order to make the halt worthwhile. Dyson trailers were better in this respect, though when they were overloaded with a 52-ton Centurion tank (introduced

just after the war) problems such as cracked cross-members arose.

The Diamond T 980, as the first model was called, went into production in 1941, and first saw active service with the British Eighth Army in North Africa. After the United States entered the war, production was stepped up to meet their needs as well, and a modified version called the 981 was introduced. This had a 500ft winch cable in place of the 980's 300ft cable and a roller in the front bumper which allowed the cable to be paid out from the front as well as the rear. This was useful for self-recovery, while the rear winch was used for hauling tanks onto the trailer. The 981 was later adopted by British forces as well, while in 1943 a wider three-seater open cab was introduced. Like similar cabs in other American trucks this could be fitted with a ring-mount for a .50 machine gun. A total of 5,871 Diamond T 980/981s were made from 1941 to the summer of 1945, and they remained in British Army service for many years. They were gradually replaced by the more powerful Thornycroft Antars, which did not prove so reliable, and the last Diamond Ts were not retired until 1973. During the 1950s many were re-

engined with Rolls-Royce C6N six-cylinder diesels. They were the mainstay of heavy haulage contractors in Britain and Western Europe for more than twenty years after the end of the war. Most were used for pulling trailers, but the Colonial Sand & Stone Co. of New York City operated a fleet of them with high-sided bodies for gravel carrying, up to the early 1970s.

On reasonable surfaces the Diamond Ts performed well, but their lack of a driven front axle made them less satisfactory off-road, where disabled tanks were quite likely to be found. This drawback led to the development of the 6x6 armoured tractor known as the Pacific M26, or more familiarly the 'Dragon Wagon'. It was designed by the Knuckey Truck Company of San Francisco, a small firm which specialised in mining and quarry trucks, and was based on one of their existing models. Powered by a six-cylinder Hall-Scott 440 engine of 17.85 litres capacity and 240bhp, it had a patented centre pivot, chain-drive to the rear bogie. The chains were oiled by a total-loss system which left a trail of drops wherever an M26 went. Transmission was by a four-speed gear-box and three-speed transfer box, with shaft-drive

Above: **A restored Diamond T 980 towing a two-axle trailer carrying an M series halftrack.** *(The Tank Museum. Bovington)*

to the front axle. The seven-man cab was fully armoured with ¾-inch plate at the front, and ¼ inch on the sides, rear and top, and with a ring-mount for a .30 or .50 machine gun. The M26 was very well equipped with winches, having one rated at 35,000 pounds at the front, and two, rated at 60,000 pounds each, behind the cab. For repairs in the field, it carried an oxy-acetylene welding unit. Overall weight of the tractor was 20½ tons, and of the combined unit 37.6 tons, and it was rated to retrieve tanks weighing up to 44 tons. However, the equipment being used at the end of the war often exceeded this, and the M26 had to cope with overloads of 12 tons or more.

The small Knuckey works did not have the capacity to make the M26 in quantity, so the production contract was given to the Pacific Car & Foundry Company of Renton, Washington, with the semi-trailers being made by Fruehauf. The armoured cab was replaced in 1944 by a soft-top version known as the M26A1. The number of occasions when recovery vehicles came under enemy fire were not many, and did not justify the extra weight and cost of all the armour. An M26A1 weighed 12.32 tons, a saving of more than 8 tons

compared with the M26. Quite apart from the extra load on the engine, very heavy units were damaging to road surfaces which were pretty poor anyway. Because of this experiments were being made at the end of the war with double-ended transporters with fewer but larger section tyres.

Just as the Diamond T was widely used by the British, the Pacific M26 was retained by the US Army for its own use, and it is believed that only one served with the British Army, out of the 1,272 units made, both armoured and soft-skinned, between 1943 and 1945. Like the Diamond Ts, the Pacifics found new careers in heavy transport after the war. Probably the most famous were the six acquired by Wynns of Newport, Monmouthshire, who fitted civilian cabs and, later, replaced the Hall-Scott engines with 15-litre Meadows units. Each bore its individual name, 'Dreadnought,' 'Conqueror,' 'Challenger,' 'Enterprise,' 'Helpmate' and 'Valiant,' and the last was not withdrawn until 1973. Pacifics were also used for heavy haulage in France and Belgium.

No other American tank transporters acheived the fame of the Diamond T or the Pacific. Federal built some 6x4 tractor/semi-trailer units powered

Right: **An M2
armoured
personnel carrier
used by Winston
Churchill, Field
Marshal
Montgomery and
Field Marshal Sir
Alan Brooke,
inspecting tanks
of the 'Desert
Rats'. The occasion
was a victory
parade in Berlin in
July 1945.**
(IWM)

by Cummins HB600 six-cylinder diesel engines, but with a 20 ton rating they were not suited to the heavier tanks in service (a Sherman 1BY weighed over 32 tons) and were more commonly used for carrying heavy engineering plant. Some were converted to drawbar tractors and used for pulling trailers loaded with 36 foot railway lines. The small Dart Truck Company of Kansas City built prototypes of 6x6 tractor/semi-trailer units with 40 tons capacity, both soft-skinned and armoured, and Mack built an experimental 'double ender,' with two 4x4 traction units, each powered by a 240bhp engine and 21x28 low pressure tyres.

Halftrack Vehicles

The best known American halftracks were the M series made as a standardised design by Autocar, Diamond T, International and White. These had a similar front end to the White M3A1 Scout Car but used more powerful engines, a 147bhp 6.3-litre White AX in the Autocar, Diamond T and White, and a 143bhp IHC in the International. They all had four-speed gearboxes with two-speed transfer boxes and drive to the front axle as well as the tracked bogie. Several variants were made, as follows:-

	Maker
M2 Armoured Personnel Carrier, 10 seats	Autocar, White
M3 Armoured Personnel Carrier 13 seats	Autocar, Diamond T, White
M4 Mortar Carrier	White
M5 Armoured Personnel Carrier, 13 seats	International
M9 Armoured Car	International
M13 Multiple Gun Carrier (two 0.50 AA machine guns in turret)	White
M14 as above	International
M15 Multiple Gun Carrier A1 (one 37mm AA gun and two .50 machine guns, all synchronised, in rotating turret)	Autocar
T12 75mm Gun Carriage	Autocar
T16 as M2, but with overhead armour and larger bogies experimental only	Autocar
T30 75mm Howitzer Carriage	White

Several of the above models could be fitted with ring-mounted .50 machine guns above the cab, in which case they bore the suffix -A1, as M2A1.

These halftracks were widely used by US forces in most theatres of the war, and were also supplied under Lend-Lease to Great Britain, Canada and the Soviet Union. A total of 41,170 were made.

Above: **This M series halftrack is being used by the CO of the Field Regimental Section of the Royal Artillery as a wireless vehicle when he was away from HQ. With one wireless working to divisional HQ and the other to the observation posts, it provided a 'step up' or relay to boost the signal over long distances.** *(IWM)*

Right: **An M13 multiple-gun carrier of the 11th Armoured Division at Travemunde, 3 May 1945. In the background are a large number of German prisoners. Other vehicles in the photo include a Jeep, Opel 1.3-litre cabriolet, Opel van and, behind the half-track, a tracked Universal Carrier.** *(IWM)*

Several other types of halftrack were made during the war, but the only one to go into production was the Allis-Chalmers Snow Tractor. Powered by a Willys Jeep engine, this was used by the Army Air Force rescue units, and could be had with wheels or skis at the front. Various types of halftrack truck were made by Autocar, Diamond T, Mack and White, but none was put into production. They included an armoured truck of which one experimental model each was made by Autocar and White, powered by a 13.3-litre flat-twelve engine, and forward control trucks by Diamond T and Mack, the latter with a rear-mounted engine.

Amphibians

Although some experimental tracked amphibians had been built during the 1920s, nothing in the way of a production vehicle appeared until just before America's entry into the War. In 1941 the ever-inventive Marmon-Herrington company built a simple hull welded from flat sheet metal, to a

design by the New York based naval architects Sparkman & Stephens. The chassis was probably a Bantam BRC (Jeep), though this cannot be positively confirmed.

The following year Ford built a generally similar vehicle, also with a Sparkman & Stephens designed hull, on their GPW (Jeep) chassis. This went into production in September 1942 under the code GPA (General Purpose, Amphibious), and about 6,000 were made over the next 13 months. The original contract was for 12,778 but the amphibious Jeep, or 'Seep' as it was nicknamed, did not live up to expectations. It could only operate in fairly calm water, and its range was very limited. Even at a water speed of 5½ mph, its range was no more than 18¾ miles, compared with 250 miles on land at a cruising speed of 40-45mph. This was due to power loss through the propeller, driven from a power-take-off on the transmission. Only two speeds were used while in the water. With an unladen weight of 3,660 pounds the GPA weighed 1,210 pounds more than an ordinary Jeep. They were mostly used for reconnaissance and liaison work with the larger DUKW amphibians, and were supplied under Lend-Lease to the British and Russian forces. The latter country made their own versions after the war, based on the GAZ-69, called the GAZ-46.

If the GPA was only a limited success, the larger DUKW was one of the most useful vehicles of the war. It was conceived by civilian engineer Roger W. Hofheins, from Buffalo, NY, whose first project was the Ford V8 engined Aqua-Cheetah with mid-mounted engine driving all four wheels by chains. Later versions used Dodge WC front and rear axles, and eventually a rear-mounted Dodge engine, but the Aqua-Cheetah was never awarded an Army contract. However, Hofheins's idea for a larger load-carrying amphibious truck was taken up by P.C. Putman of the NDRC (National Defence Research Committee) and a prototype was ordered from General Motors and Sparkman & Stephens. This was built initially on the GMC AFKWX 353 forward-control chassis, with hull designed by Roderick Stephens Jr.

The Army was unenthusiastic about the project to start with, mainly because in 1942 they were not aware of the problems involved in landing large numbers of men and supplies without any harbour facilities. It is said that a change of heart came when a prototype amphibious truck went to the rescue of a Coast Guard boat which was sinking off Cape Cod, Massachusetts. The sea was so rough that lifeboats were unable to help, but the truck, crewed by Putman and Stephens, succeeded in taking off the crew and bringing them to land in six minutes. Whether the Army really based a major purchasing decision on one incident is open to doubt, but anyway it is a good story.

Right and below:
US Army halftracks in action. Most of these were built by White, though the work was also contracted to Autocar, Diamond T and International. Top is a 1942 T 12 75mm gun carriage, made by Autocar. Bottom is a White M5-A1 armoured personnel carrier on the beach after landing at Les Andalouses, Algeria in 1943.

In October 1942 an initial order for 2,000 6x6 amphibious trucks was placed. The chassis was now the normal-control CCKW 353, and the amphibious version was coded by General Motors DUKW (D = 1942, U = amphibian, K = all-wheel drive, W = dual rear axles). It was immediately, and inevitably, nicknamed 'the Duck,' and as such it has been known ever since. It was a massive vehicle, 31 feet long and 8ft 3ins wide, and weighing over 15,000 pounds. Maximum load was 5,000 pounds or 2¼ tons, which was only a little lower than the 2½ tons of the ordinary CCKW 353, and as a personnel carrier the DUKW could carry up to 40 troops. Pressure in the 11x18 tyres could be varied from a panel on the dashboard, in front of the driver's seat. Optional equipment included a 105mm Howitzer M2A1 with a pitch indicator to give the crew at least some help towards accurate firing while the DUKW was rocking about on the water. A 4.5mm rocket launcher capable of firing 120 rounds in a few seconds could be incorporated, and experiments were made with sails to enable the vehicles to make silent approaches, assuming a favourable wind.

The DUKW first saw active service during the New Caledonia (Pacific) landings of the US Army in March 1943, followed by the North Africa landings shortly afterwards. The British Eighth Army used 230 DUKWs during the invasion of Sicily in July 1943, bringing the total used by allied forces in

Below: **A GMC CCKW-353 straddles two DUKWs, which used the same running gear. Most DUKWs were armed personnel carriers, though they could carry a 105mm Howitzer when used for beach assaults. Generally, they would not be fired while the DUKW was in the water, as pitching and rolling rendered any kind of accuracy impossible.** *(The Tank Museum, Bovington)*

that operation to around a thousand. Their task was to ferry troops and supplies of all kinds, including food and medicine, from the landing ships to the beaches where, once a bridgehead had been established, the cargo would be taken inland by ordinary trucks. However, the DUKWs were sometimes sent inland themselves, causing severe traffic jams when their drivers tried to manoeuvre the monsters around the narrow lanes. During the Normandy landings more than 2,000 DUKWs were used, those in the British sector alone carrying more than 10,000 tons per day. A total 3,050,000 tons was brought ashore in France and Belgium between 6 June 1944 and 8 May 1945. In the Pacific and in Burma they were also invaluable; during a 72 hour period 6,000 men and 200 vehicles were carried, in DUKWs, across the Irrawaddy River, which is four times the width of the Rhine.

A total of 21,147 DUKWs were built, and they remained in service with the armies of the United States, Canada, Britain and the Soviet Union for many years. In addition they were supplied to the post-war armies of France, Holland, Belgium and West Germany, helping in flood disasters and performing many other useful duties. The Russians built their own version on the ZIL-151 chassis, with one very important improvement over the American model, an unloading ramp at the rear which did away with the need for a hoisting derrick or crane to take off supplies. The last nine DUKWs of the British Army's Royal Corps of Transport were not retired until 1974.

Above: **Underside of a DUKW showing the drive to the front axle and semi-elliptical leaf springs.** (*The Tank Museum, Bovington*)

Right: **Cockpit of a DUKW. The instructions on the right-hand side are about engaging and disengaging of the front axle.** (*The Tank Museum, Bovington*)

Above and left:
Two examples of the GMC DUKW 6x6 amphibian, during the landing at Hollandia, New Guinea in 1943. The crane for loading/unloading was a necessity as the DUKW had no ramp, a deficiency put right by the Russians with their version on the ZIL-151 chassis.
(IWM)

CHAPTER FIVE

Soviet Union

Both in fighting and supply vehicles, Russia was
desperately short of suitable transport.

The Soviet motor industry did not begin to grow until the First Five Year Plan of 1928 to 1933. This period saw the expansion of the AMO factory in Moscow, which made 1½-ton trucks of Fiat type, and, more importantly, the establishment of the GAZ factory in Gorky in 1932. When the building of the factory began the town still bore its old name of Nizhni Novgorod, but in 1932 it was changed in honour of the famous writer Maxim Gorky who was born there. The factory was built with financial and material help from Ford, the architect being Albert Kahn who was responsible for the River Rouge plant near Detroit. With a site area of 256 acres and a workforce of 12,000 it was claimed to be the biggest motor factory in Europe. Its products were almost identical to Fords made in America and elsewhere, the Model AA 1½-ton truck, followed by the Model A car, made almost exclusively in open tourer form. The rapid growth of the GAZ factory helped to increase total vehicle output from 50,000 during the first Five Year Plan to more than 200,000 during the second. Other factories which contributed vehicles included ZIS (Zavod Imieni Stalin) and YAG (Yaroslavl Automobilni Zavod).

Soviet Russia's motorisation programme was intended to improve communications and increase the production of food from the land, and little attention was given to its military potential. There were no specifically military trucks or tractors, though many of the designs could be adapted to the needs of the armed services without too much dif-

ficulty. The Nazi-Soviet Pact of 1939 made Russia feel safe from invasion, so when 164 divisions of Hitler's forces crossed the frontier at numerous points between the Baltic and the Black Sea on 22 June 1941, she was, if not totally unprepared, certainly at a very grave disadvantage.

Both in fighting and supply vehicles, Russia was desperately short of suitable transport and, without the massive aid provided by the allies in the West, the victorious sweep of the Soviet Army from Stalingrad to Berlin would have been much less certain, and might never have taken place at all. As it was, the USA alone provided military equipment valued at $9,119,204,000 which included more than 400,000 trucks as well as tanks, scout cars and artillery tractors. This is not to denigrate in any way the courage and tenacity of the Russian soldiers and civilians in tying down more than 160 German divisions which would otherwise have been free to attack the Allies.

As the war progressed the Russian motor industry did develop more modern machines such as the GAZ-67 Jeep, but they never had a 4x4 or 6x6 truck, so relied on British and American vehicles of this type. Since the 1950s the Soviet Army has been equipped with a wide range of cross-country cars and trucks.

Staff Cars

The most widely used staff cars of the Soviet Army were Ford-based products of the Gorky factory.

The GAZ-A was made from 1932 to 1936, during which time a total of nearly 42,000 were built. They were very similar in design and appearance to the American Ford Model A, with 3280cc four-cylinder side-valve engines and four wheel mechanical brakes. They were almost all open tourers, which is curious in view of the severe climate in much of Russia, but apparently the GAZ people never acquired the dies for saloon cars. A few were coachbuilt by a company called Aremkuzov in Moscow, but it is not known if any of these entered military service. The GAZ-A was succeeded in 1936 by the more modern looking GAZ M-1 which had a four-door saloon body resembling that of a 1934 American Ford. The engine was still the faithful Model A, with compression ratio increased from 4.2 to 4.6:1, and power up from 42 to 50bhp. Made from 1936 to 1941, the M-1 was widely used as a staff car during the war, supplemented by the GAZ-11-40 which was similar but used a 76bhp 3480cc six-cylinder engine. This was seen in tourer as well as saloon form, and had a 4x4 variant, the GAZ-61. The 11-40 had a top speed of 75mph, while the 61 could reach 62mph on the road and had a satisfactory cross-country performance, although the traditional Ford-type transverse leaf suspension must have given passengers a pretty swaying ride.

The top brass in the Soviet Army were allocated examples of the ZIS-101 limousine. Introduced in 1936 this was a large car on American lines, powered by a 90bhp 5750cc ohv straight-eight engine.

The wheelbase was 11ft 9in and unladen weight 2550kg. These cars were made in larger numbers than the post-war ZIS-110 and ZIL-111, with 1,294 being turned out in 1937, and were used as taxis in addition to being sold or given as presents to professional men as well as senior members of the Communist Party and army officers. A rare model was the ZIS-102 open tourer, also used as a staff car. This and the 101 could be fitted with aluminium pistons in place of cast iron, which raised output to 110bhp, while a downdraught carburettor introduced in 1940 gave an additional 6bhp.

Among the vehicles supplied to the Soviet Army by the Americans was the Jeep, and in 1943 the GAZ plant began to produce a 4x4 field car on similar lines, known as the GAZ-67. It was slightly heavier than its American counterpart, at 2910 pounds compared with 2450 pounds for the standard Jeep, but overall dimensions were pretty close. The GAZ-67 was powered by the familiar four-cylinder Ford Model A engine which developed about the same power (54bhp) as the smaller Jeep engine. Its acceleration was not as good as the Jeep's, but it had good off-road performance and the reliability of the engine was excellent.

About 200 GAZ-67 or 67Bs were imported into America from Czechoslovakia or Yugoslavia in 1966, to provide spare parts for owners of Model A Fords, and the quality of the block castings, crank-shafts, etc, was found to be excellent. It was thought that Russian and Swedish steel was of a higher quality than US steel, because of the lower proportion

Above: **The front end of the GAZ-AAA was identical to that of the Ford Model A, but the rear double driving axles with remarkable articulation were never seen in Detroit. It was made from 1934 to 1943, and from 1938 used the GAZ M1 3285cc four-cylinder engine. It had a two-range four-speed gearbox. The civilian-type GS body illustrated was the common style, but the AAA was also seen in ambulance, command car or anti-aircraft gun carrier forms.**
(L Suslavicius Collection)

of scrap metal that went into it. On the other hand the fuel tanks were made of thinner plate than those of the American Ford, which seems rather an unwise economy in a vehicle which was to be used in battle.

In 1945 a modified version was introduced and known as the GAZ-67B, distinguished from its predecessor by a wider track of 4ft 9in compared with 4ft 1in. This was made in large numbers up to 1953 when it was replaced by the larger and more modern GAZ-69A. The 67B was made in greater numbers than the 67, and many were used in the Korean War of 1950-1953. The few examples existing in the West are all 67Bs captured in Korea.

Trucks

All the Russian-built trucks used in World War Two were of civilian origin, the most widespread models coming from the GAZ and ZIS factories. GAZ trucks were made in a variety of models, all based on the Ford Model AA 1½-ton chassis. The original GAZ-AA was built from 1932 to 1938 when it was succeeded by the GAZ-MM which had the more powerful 50bhp, M-1 engine but was otherwise similar in design. The MM differed in appearance by having squared-off mudguards which were cheaper to make and easier to clean, whereas the AA had the rounded type of the original American design. The AA and MM were mostly fitted with open dropside bodies, but they

were also made as vans, light buses and ambulances. Like most Soviet trucks, they could be had with producer gas or sometimes compressed gas equipment.

For heavier loads the GAZ factory made the AAA, a 6x4 truck rated for a 2½ ton carrying capacity. This was no longer than the AA, but the additional axle spread the load and the fact that it was powered gave better traction over rough ground. The normal body was an open dropside truck, but the AAA chassis was also used to carry a quadruple 7.62mm Maxim machine gun for anti-aircraft duties, or as a nine-stretcher ambulance. The BA-10 armoured car was built on the AAA chasis. Early AAAs, made from 1933 to 1938, had the Model A engine, later ones using the more powerful M-1. Production figures for GAZ trucks are not known for certain, but total Soviet truck and bus production between 1931 and 1940 has been estimated at 1,020,900 of which probably 70% came from the GAZ factory or the KIM factory in Moscow which manufactured the same design. The GAZ-MM was made up to 1948.

The other widely used Russian truck was the ZIS-5, made at the Moscow factory which began life under the name AMO. Between 1924 and 1932 they made about 6,000 of the AMO-15, a Fiat-based 1½-ton truck which was used by the army as well as in civilian life. This was joined in 1931 by the AMO-3, a larger truck based on an American International Harvester pattern, with a 60bhp 4880cc six-cylinder engine of Hercules design.

Although the Russians were forced to copy other designs, they generally chose the best! In 1932 the AMO plant was renamed ZIS (Zavod Imieni Stalin) and the AMO-3 became the ZIS-3. Two years later it became the ZIS-5, of similar design but with a 73bhp 5550cc engine. A characteristic of both models was the windscreen divided about two thirds of the way across instead of in the centre, so that the driver had a wider field of vision than his passenger. These sturdy trucks remained in production until 1955 in the Urals factory, built in 1941/42 when the German advance threatened Moscow. A large number of ZIS-5s were supplied to the Republican Army in the Spanish Civil War (1936-39) and were sold to civilian users afterwards. They were by no means a rare sight in Spain up to the mid-1960s. Spaniards nicknamed them 'Tres Hermanos Communistas', ('Three Communist Brothers') because the Cyrillic letters embossed on the radiator header tank read 3HC. The ZIS-5 chassis was used for carrying searchlights, pontoon bridging equipment, tankers, snowploughs, air compressors and other special purpose vehicles. Later models, and probably all those made in the Urals factory, had flat topped mudguards like the GAZ-MMs.

There were several variants on the basic ZIS-5 design, including the ZIS-32 4x4 truck of 1941 and the ZIS-6 6x4 of 1935-45. The latter was used for carrying rocket launching equipment. Capable of firing 16 rockets in 8 to 10 seconds, these were nicknamed 'Stalin Organ Pipes' because of their appearance, and were also mounted on foreign chassis such as the Ford WOT8 or Studebaker 6x6. ZIS also made two models of halftrack truck described on page 179.

Heavier trucks were built by the YAG (Yaroslavl Automobilni Zavod) factory at Yaroslavl on the Volga. This was set up on Lenin's orders in 1924 at the same time as the AMO plant in Moscow and the first YA3 trucks used the 4.4-litre four-cylinder AMO engine. It was succeeded in 1928 by the heavier YA4 powered by a 7-litre six-cylinder Daimler-Benz engine, followed by the YAG-4 of 1934-36 which had a 5550cc ZIS engine. Both these models were still in use by the Soviet Army during the war, as was the 6x4 YAG-10 powered by a six-cylinder, Hercules engine. Like other Russian 6x4 trucks, this could carry an anti-aircraft gun.

A more unusual design to come from the Yaroslavl factory was the YAG-12, an 8x8 truck with a load capacity of 12 tons. This was powered by a 7020cc six-cylinder Continental engine, either imported complete from America or assembled in Russia. It was unusual in combining twin-steering axles with a bonnetted engine, most twin-steering trucks being of cab over engine layout. Details of the drive system are not known, but it was certainly very advanced at a time when 8x8s were hardly known anywhere in the world. (The Guy 8x8 artillery tractor of 1931 never went into production, while the American Army used no

Above: **Much rarer than the GAZ-AAA was the GAZ-33 6x6 truck powered by a slightly larger engine of 3480cc and six cylinders. Like the AAA it had a two-range gearbox giving eight forward speeds and was built for a 2000kg payload. Only prototypes were made.**
(L Suslavicius Collection)

8x8s until after the war). One photograph shows tracks over the rear wheels. The YAG-12 was nominally in production from 1932 to 1941, but probably not all that many were made.

Halftracks

Russia had a long tradition of interest in halftrack vehicles stretching back to Czarist days when the Frenchman Adolphe Kégresse was the manager of the Imperial garages. At least one Packard Twin-Six belonging to Nicholas II was fitted with halftracks and skis under the front wheels, while Lenin used a similarly-equipped Rolls-Royce Silver Ghost. In the 1930s halftrack conversions were made on GAZ-M1 cars and pickups, GAZ MM trucks and ZIS-5 trucks. The M1s were equipped with Nati-type bogies and fitted with either saloon bodies or pick-ups, both types having a load capacity of 12cwt. The latter were called by the Russians 'Pikaps' or 'Vezdekhods' (go anywhere). The halftrack version of the MM truck was known as the GAZ-60, and had a capacity of 1¼ tons and a top speed of 22mph.

ZIS made two models of halftrack truck. The ZIS-33 retained the twin rear wheels of the ordinary truck, but had sprockets to the fore and aft of them to carry the tracks. The later ZIS-42 had conventional tracks on the Somua principle and

carried a payload of 2¼ tons. It was in production from 1942 to 1944.

Artillery Tractors

Unlike other countries the Soviet Union made widespread use of fully-tracked tractors for hauling their heavy artillery. By the 1930s such vehicles were already being built in various sizes for agricultural work and needed little alteration to make them suitable for artillery traction. They were better suited to the prevailing conditions of snow and mud than wheeled tractors and, as many soldiers had been brought up on farms, they were already familiar with this type of vehicle.

The Stalinets-65 was a large, agricultural type tractor powered by a six-cylinder diesel engine, with a weight of 11 tons and a drawbar pull of 30 tons. Like most military tractors it had a closed cab. Other vehicles such as the Stalin and Komintern were tractor-trucks with a load carrying area behind their cabs. These could carry crew and ammunition as well as tow guns, and were more practical than the Stalinets type. A smaller forward control tractor-truck was the STZ5-2B with 7460cc four-cylinder engine, derived from the STZ-NAT1 1TA tractor. Both used the Nati suspension system with horizontal coil springs and oscillating bogies.

Above: **Another variant on the ZIS-5 was a halftrack version the ZIS-42. Payload was 2½ tons on roads and 1.7 cross-country.** *(L Suslavicius Collection)*

Left above: **Derived from the YAG-10 6x4 was the YAG-12 with drive to all eight wheels and a load capacity of 12 tons. It had a top speed of 28 mph.** *(L Suslavicius Collection)*

Left bottom: **ZIS-5s built in the Urals factory from 1941 mostly had flat topped wings These were standard on the ZIS-5V which also had a wooden cab and no front brakes.** *(Nick Georgano)*

CHAPTER SIX

France

French Army units went into war in vehicles that
had been built for service in World War One.

L ike Great Britain, France did not pay a great
deal of attention to military vehicles until
shortly before World War Two, so there was
little of the energetic development that went
on across the Rhine from the early 1930s onwards.
The French relied much too heavily on requisitioned civilian vehicles, and many of these were
old, as truck production fell from 40,000 in 1930 to
barely 20,000 in 1938. During the same period,
Italy and the United States doubled their production, and Germany increased hers six fold. Only in
December 1936 did Defence Minister Edouard
Daladier order a 14 million Franc re-armament
programme which included 3,200 modern tanks
and 5,000 smaller tracked vehicles. In fact a number
of French Army units went to war in vehicles that
had been built for the first conflict, particularly the
sturdy Berliet CBA 4 ton truck.

A field in which a lot of valuable work was done
was that of the halftrack vehicle, which was first
made a practical proposition by Adolphe Kégresse
in the early 1920s. The French industry also built a
number of advanced all-wheel drive vehicles with
two and three axles, produced as part of the
Daladier programme.

The German Army did not launch its attack on
France until 10 May 1940, and 35 days later they
entered Paris. The British Expeditionary Force had
been evacuated at Dunkirk leaving behind all their
vehicles and other heavy equipment, and organised
French resistance did not continue beyond the end
of June. Consequently the period during which
they were engaged in active service was extremely
short, but the variety of vehicles at their disposal
was considerable, and worth studying. Also,
French-built vehicles made a valuable addition to
the German transport fleet, not only the thousands
which were captured, but those that were produced
in French factories.

Staff Cars

A variety of civilian models was acquired by the
French Army, unmodified apart from carrying military insignia and flag mountings in some cases.
They were divided into two classes, voiture de liaison de moins de 15CV, and voiture de liaison de
plus de 15CV (communications car of less than
15hp and more than 15hp). It should be remem-
bered that the French unit of horsepower is larger
than the British, so 15CV is equivalent to about
22hp. Among the more widely used cars in the first
category were the Citroën 11CV front-wheel
drive, Renault Prima-Quatre and Peugeot 402B,
while larger cars included the big six-cylinder
Renault Viva Grand Sport and Vivastella, also the
Matford V8 and Hotchkiss 680. French forces in
Algeria and Morocco also used various older models of Citroën with rear-wheel drive. These
included an open command car on modified C4-G
four-cylinder or C6 six-cylinder chassis. Both had
specially enlarged radiator header tanks to cope
with the hot climate and oversize tyres.

Field Cars

To complement the ordinary road going cars just mentioned, the French used a variety of ingenious purpose-built field cars, of roughly the same size and purpose as the Dodge 15cwt command car. Their ancestor was the 6x4 Renault Model MH, several of which were used in successful crossings of the Sahara in the 1920s. Whereas André Citroën favoured the Kégresse halftrack system for traction on soft ground, his great rival Louis Renault preferred wheels with double tyres all round. The French Army bought 22 of these Renaults in 1929, and at least one was acquired by the Royal Army Service Corps for evaluation. Renault themselves did not pursue the idea of the cross-country car, but it was taken up by three truck makers, Berliet, Laffly and Latil.

The Berliets were made in 4x4, 6x4 and 6x6 models, powered by 50bhp four-cylinder (VUDB4) or 60bhp six-cylinder (VURB2) engines. The prototype 4x4 of 1928 was rear-engined, but production models had front-mounted engines and four-speed gearboxes with two-speed transfer boxes, giving a total of eight forward and two reverse speeds. Power was transmitted from the transfer box by individual shafts to each wheel. A total of 53 of the six-cylinder cars were built in 1929-30, one of which was sold to the King of the Belgians.

The four-cylinder 4x4 field car was introduced in 1932. It was of similar appearance and size to the six, both cars carrying their spare wheels on idler hubs between the front and rear axles. These wheels were sufficiently low to support the vehicle and prevent the chassis from getting stuck at the top of a very steep incline. The 6x4 and 6x6 Berliet field cars were made in very limited numbers.

The 6x6 VPB was the first to appear, in 1936. It had a 50bhp six-cylinder engine and an unusual drive system by which power was transmitted from the front-mounted engine to a central differential in the rear axle, and thence by twin propeller shafts to the central and front axles. The axles were spread equally, so that the middle one was halfway along the chassis and not in a bogie with the rear axle as in most six-wheeled vehicles. The 6x4 Berliet VPDS did have a normal rear bogie, though the axles were well spaced apart. It also had two tiny wheels below the front door to prevent grounding on rough surfaces.

Laffly was an old-established company from Asnieres, near Paris, which specialised in fire engines on their own and other makers' chassis. In 1936 they produced a 4x4 cross-country field car powered by a Peugeot engine. Production models from 1937 to 1940 used the 2.3-litre four-cylinder Hotchkiss 486 engine and in fact quite a lot of complete cars were built by Hotchkiss to the Laffly design. Some were also made by La Licorne. The V15 R, as the production model was called, was a substantial looking five/six-seater open car with large section 230x40 tyres and two small bumper

Above: **The Laffly S35T 6x6 artillery tractor used the largest of the make's engines, a 6230cc 100bhp four-cylinder. Drive was via a four-speed gearbox and two-speed transfer box. Towing capacity was 12 tons. Many were captured by the Wehrmacht and used on the eastern front under the name Schwerer Radschlepper (f) Laffly S35T.** *(Bart Vanderveen Collection)*

wheels at the front to protect the radiator and prevent the car from digging its nose into the ground. It had permanently engaged four-wheel drive, a four-speed gearbox with two-speed transfer box and shaft drive to lockable differentials on front and rear axles. It had a top speed of 50mph on good roads. Although a number of field cars were built, the design was more widely used as the V15T light artillery tractor, while Laffly also made heavier 6x6 tractors (see page 184). Some 6x6 chassis carried field car bodywork as well.

The third French manufacturer who made 4x4 field cars was Latil, better known for their heavy 4x4 tractors which had seen widespread military and civilian use since World War One. Their field car was called the M7T1 and was built on substantial light truck lines. The gross vehicle weight was 3 tons, compared with just under $2\frac{3}{4}$ tons for the Laffly V15R. The engine was a 55bhp 2720cc four-cylinder Latil-built unit, driving through a

four-speed gearbox and two-speed transfer box. Brakes were power-assisted hydraulic and the car had coil-spring independent suspension all round. It could seat six passengers with a locker for ammunition or other equipment behind them, and was fitted with a rear-mounted winch of 2.2 tons capacity. There was also an Air Force version with a four-door estate car body known as a Break d' Aviation.

The Lorraine company of Argenteuil, a branch of the famous de Dietrich engineering concern, built cross-country vehicles of Tatra design from 1934 to 1940. Among these was a light 6x4 chassis on which some field car bodies were built. It had a 2-litre flat-four cylinder air-cooled engine and the typical Tatra tubular backbone frame, with independent suspension on all six wheels. Like the Laffly, it had bumper wheels at the front.

Altogether the French cross-country cars and tractors or VTT – Voiture Tous Terrains as they were called, were well engineered and advanced

machines. It was a tragedy that they were not available in larger numbers and with greater manpower. As it was many of them never saw active service, so rapid was the German advance in May/June 1940, as they were captured to become valuable additions to the Wehrmacht's fleet.

Trucks

Most of the French Army trucks used for general carrying of personnel and goods were of civilian design, with little modification apart from front towing hooks so that they could be easily extricated from trouble by other vehicles. Among the types supplied to the army during the 1930s were most of the well known trucks such as the Citroën 23, 32 and 45, Renaults from $1\frac{1}{2}$ to $4\frac{1}{2}$ tons, Matford V8 5-6 ton, Panhard 5 ton, Latil M2B1 $1\frac{1}{2}$ ton and FB6 $3\frac{1}{2}$ ton and Peugeot DK5 1.4 ton. Suppliers of six-wheel vehicles included Berliet, Bernard, Renault and Willeme. As well as ordinary drop sided or canvas tilt bodies, these trucks carried special coachwork for use as radio vans, mobile workshops, photographic laboratories, etc. Most had petrol engines, though diesels were available in the larger Citroëns and Renaults, and also in the Berliets and Bernards. Producer-gas units were also employed in many French army trucks, as they had been in their civilian versions.

After the fall of France a number of firms were put to work making vehicles for the Germans. Prominent among these was Renault, which turned out several thousand trucks, mostly the AH series, a forward-control model with sloping front which was continued after the war. These included the $2\frac{1}{2}$-ton AHS, $3\frac{1}{2}$-ton AHN and 5-ton AHR. By 1944 rubber was in such short supply that some of these Renaults were delivered with iron tyres.

Louis Renault's efficiency at truck production led to charges of collaboration which were not strictly fair as he was simply trying to keep his factories going and his employees in work. However, he made a grave error in not turning over exclusively to truck production in 1939-40, when he

Far left: **The Laffly V15R had a much lower profile than the R15R (below), and used the same Hotchkiss engine. As well as the reconnaissance car shown, it was made as the V15T tractor for 25mm anti-tank guns.** *(Bart Vanderveen Collection)*

Left: **The Latil M7T1 was introduced in 1939, with an order for 400. As well as the open command car shown, it was made with a closed estate-type body, the Break d'Aviation, for the Air Force, and as a tractor. A further batch of 300 was made after the war.** *(Bart Vanderveen Collection)*

Below: **The Laffly R15R was a 4x4 powered by a 2.4-litre four-cylinder Hotchkiss engine. This is a command car, but there were also reconnaissance car versions with cutaway doors.** *(Bart Vanderveen Collection)*

could have supplied large numbers of vehicles to the French Army. Instead he continued with car production, thinking the war would be over in a year or two, so that when his factories eventually turned over to trucks alone, they all went to the German Army. For this error he paid with his life, dying in mysterious circumstances in the Fresne prison in October 1944.

Other companies which made trucks in quantity for the Germans were Peugeot, who built 48,813, mostly the DK5 which used the cab and front end of the 402 passenger car, mated with a van or tilt body and twin rear wheels, and Citroën, who built over 15,000 of their model 32. The Wehrmacht also used Citroën models 23R and 45 but these were not made under the occupation. Latil also made a number of 4x4 heavy tractors for use on the Eastern Front.

Apart from the trucks mentioned so far, most of the more specialised vehicles were of the same family as the tractors described in the next section. One which fell between the two categories, conventional truck and tractor, was the Latil M2TL6. This was a normal looking bonnetted 2-ton truck, but had four-wheel drive to help it when good roads were not available. It could be fitted with a Latil 70bhp petrol engine or a Gardner diesel.

Artillery Tractors

France had a long tradition of building 4x4 tractors, dating back to just before World War One. The leading makers of such vehicles during the war were Latil, Panhard and Renault and by the end of the conflict there were something like 2,000 Latils and 700 Renaults in service. Latil made a speciality of the 4x4 tractor between the wars and they were widely used for heavy haulage in France and also in Britain, where they were made under licence by Shelvoke & Drewry from 1932 to 1937. Some had four-wheel steering and there were also forestry tractor and road/rail versions.

The French Army used two basic models of Latil tractor in the 1930s, the TL and KTL light artillery tractor, and the TARH heavy artillery tractor. The former was similar to the civilian models popular on both sides of the Channel, and had a 3.3-litre four-cylinder engine six-speed gearbox, lockable differential and drive and steering on all four wheels. The TARH was a much heavier machine whose ancestry dated back to the TAR 4x4 tractor of World War One. This had a dashboard radiator and Renault-style bonnet, and was the inspiration for the American Walter tractor/truck. During the 1920s the radiator was moved to the front (on the TAR 3) and the cab became enclosed (TAR 5). Pneumatic tyres made their appearance on the TARH of 1932, the model

most widely in use at the beginning of World War Two. This had a 6080cc 68bhp four-cylinder engine and six-speed gearbox and weighed over 6½ tons. Unlike the smaller Latils, it did not have four-wheel steering. Quite a number of TARHs were captured by the Germans who found them to be of very high quality.

After the fall of France the Latil factory at Suresnes came under the control of Daimler Benz AG. Tractors were made for the Wehrmacht, including a special Eastern Front model, the FTARH. This had large metal wheels of about 150cm diameter, with steel strip spokes or rod-type spokes with hinged studs which could be swung onto the wheel treads to give increased traction, or folded round the hub when not in use. The FTARH was similar to the Porsche-designed Skoda-built Radschlepper Ost and was intended for the same work, hauling heavy artillery on the Russian front. It is not known how many were made.

The French Army also used a number of 6x6 artillery tractors, mostly by Laffly and Latil, which were similar in concept to these firms' 4x4 field cars already described. The smaller Lafflys used the same 2.3-litre four-cylinder Hotchkiss engines which powered the field cars, with four-speed gearboxes in conjunction with dual-range transfer boxes. Drive was by individual propeller shafts and there was independent suspension on all six wheels. Like the field cars, these tractors had bumper wheels at the front of the chassis and some had similar sized auxiliary wheels just behind the front axle. As a tractor it was known as the S15T, and variants included the S15L ambulance and the low profile W15T tractor or 2-ton truck. The tractors were used for towing a 47mm field gun. Like the field cars, they were made under licence by Hotchkiss as well as by Laffly.

There was also a larger Hotchkiss-powered model, the S20TL, which could be used as a tractor, 3-ton truck, radio van or tanker. Still larger versions used Laffly engines of 3450 or 6230cc (S25T, S35T, S45T) and were used for towing 105 or 155mm artillery, or general loads of 12 tons. These Lafflys were very advanced vehicles and some were bought by the armies of Afghanistan, Greece and Persia during the 1930s. Alas, they did not have much chance to serve the French Army and many were captured and put to use by the Wehrmacht.

Latil made the M7TZ and M2TZ 6x6 tractors, the former being derived from the M7T1 field car, and using the same 50bhp 2724cc four-cylinder engine. It had accommodation for a crew of four, with ammunition lockers, and normally towed a 47mm gun. The M2TZ was a larger machine with 70bhp 4084cc engine capable of towing an 8 ton load. It was made as an artillery tractor or as a recovery truck with block and tackle hoist and optional 5-ton hoist. In 1939 Latil built a prototype of a

Above: **A Latil M2TL6 artillery tractor with four-wheel drive and steering. It has a 3-ton winch and a towing capacity of 5 tons. Made in 1939, it served with the Belgian Army.**
(Vehicle displayed at the Victory Memorial Museum)

Left: **This 6x6 artillery tractor is a Laffly design, the W15T, made by Hotchkiss. A low-profile version of the S15T, its main purpose was to tow a 47mm gun, but it could also be used as a GS truck. Note the auxiliary wheels at the front to prevent bedding down on steep inclines.**
(Vehicle displayed at the Victory Memorial Museum)

remarkable 8x8 artillery tractor, with four equally spaced axles, the front and rear axles being steered. It was powered by a 140bhp 11.2-litre six-cylinder engine and carried a 10-ton winch. Only one prototype was made.

The other French company to make a six-wheeled tractor was Lorraine. Like the smaller field car, the Lorraine 28 was built under licence from Tatra. The chassis was the typical tubular backbone construction with swinging half-axles at the rear, but the engine was Lorraine's own, a 55bhp 4717cc unit. Bumper wheels were used at the front, two on each side, and drive was to the rear axles only. Lorraine also made a large 6x4 tanker under Tatra licence, with 11.2-litre engine and carrying a 9000-litre tank.

Halftracks

Between the wars France was one of the leading countries in the development of halftracked vehicles, thanks to Adolphe Kégresse. French-born Kégresse had spent much of his early life in Russia where he was manager of the Czar's garages. He produced his earliest halftracks on the royal cars, including a Packard V-12, Delaunay Belleville and Rolls-Royce Silver Ghost, the latter being subsequently used by Lenin. After the Revolution he returned to France where he found encourage-ment and financial backing from the industrialist Jacques Hinstin. Although Hinstin did make a light car under his own name he decided that a bigger manufacturer was needed if the Kégresse system was to be exploited successfully, and approached André Citroën. The first Citroën car equipped with Kégresse halftracked bogies was a B2 tourer of 1922. A number of these were made and one was acquired, for tests, by the British Army. There is a well known photograph of Queen Mary enjoying an adventurous ride in this vehicle.

An early Citroën Kégresse made the first auto-mobile crossing of the Sahara Desert (December 1922-January 1923) and they were used for other long-distance journeys such as Colomb Bechar to Tanananarive (1925-6) and the trans-Asian Yellow Cruise of 1931-32. Civilian uses of the halftracks included hotel buses in Alpine districts and towing tractors for canal barges, while the military applications were equally diverse. These included command cars, artillery tractors, vehicle recovery tractors, telephone and engineers' trucks, anti-air-craft-gun carriers and aircraft tugs. On the early models the rear axle of the bogie drove the tracks which powered the front axle by friction, but from 1927 onwards the front axle was driven and the chains drove both axles via sprockets. From 1928 onwards most Citroën-Kégresse vehicles used the 2442cc six-cylinder C6a engine.

Below: **A Unic TU1 halftrack which served as a transport truck and light artillery tractor. It is a low-profile version of the P107, and was fitted with the 2150cc four-cylinder engine from Unic's U4 passenger car. It is in the livery of the 23rd Infantry Division of the Wehrmacht who used many of the Unic halftracks.** *(Vehicle displayed at the Victory Memorial Museum)*

Above: **A Unic P107 halftrack artillery tractor requisitioned by the Germans and in service at the Russian Front.**
(NMM)

When André Citroën's company was taken over by tyre makers Michelin in 1934, Adolphe Kégresse left and formed his own consulting firm, S.E.K. (la Société d'Exploitation Kégresse), in partnership with this nephew Gustave Kégresse and an engineer named Grangerard. They sold the patents for halftracks to the Unic company of Puteaux, Seine, and in 1937 the prototypes of the Unic Type P107 were ready for testing. They were larger than the Citroëns, being powered by a 60bhp four-cylinder engine of 3454cc, with five-speed gearboxes.

The first models were inteded to be equipped with Swiss-made Oerlikon machine guns, but these turned out to have a system of mountings as used in the German Army rather than that standardised by the French! Production models of the P107 were not machine-gun equipped, but were intended to pull 75mm field guns. Manufacture began in November 1938, and was supposed to reach 15 tractors per day. However, strikes among suppliers prevented this figure from ever being attained and only 3,276 were made up to the fall of France in June 1940.

The artillery tractor had accommodation for a crew of six and an ammunition locker, while there was also a truck version for 2 ton loads or for pulling pontoon bridge trailers. Some were sent to Norway and after the evacuation found their way to Camberley where they were used for driving instruction by the Alsace Lorraine batallion of the Free French Forces. Others went to North Africa where they were again used by the Free French until replaced by American halftracks in 1943. Many were captured by the Germans who renamed them leichter Zugkraftwagen U (f) Typ 107, and

employed them on the Russian and North African fronts, and also in Normandy. Here some of them were 'repatriated' by the Allies, and, with their black crosses replaced by the tricolour, saw service once more against the Wehrmacht.

The last Kégresse design for Unic was the TU1, a low profile personnel carrier/artillery tractor powered by the 2150cc four-cylinder engine used in the Unic U4 passenger car. The canvas roof over the cab was only 4ft 3in from the ground, making it a precursor of the low profile vehicles developed by the Americans during the war.

Unfortunately the TU1 came too late to help the French; introduced in March 1940, only 236 were made before Paris fell, though quite a number were subsequently made under German occupation, both for the Wehrmacht and for civilian users such as the Toulon fire brigade.

The other company to make halftracks in quantity was Somua, a heavy truck and bus manufacturer which had originally been the vehicle division of the massive Schneider engineering combine. Their MCG truck/tractor was powered by a 60bhp four-cylinder engine and first appeared in 1932. It had a canvas tilt body for carrying crew and more powerful versions were made later, the 85bhp MCL 5 and the 110bhp six-cylinder MSCL 5. The latter was used for towing four-wheeled 155mm gun carriages. The MCL 5 was also available as a heavy recovery tractor. The final Somua halftrack was the MCJ 5, a low profile artillery tractor intended to tow a 47mm gun. The prototype was built in 1937 and 160 were ordered, with production due to start in 1940. However, the order was cancelled, possibly because of the advent of the Unic TU 1.

CHAPTER SEVEN

Italy

To prepare for campaigns in Ethiopia and Albania,
Mussolini ordered a great rearmament programme.

Although Italy entered the war nine months later than Britain, France and Germany, in June 1940, she had acquired considerable experience of warfare in the previous five years, thanks to campaigns in Ethiopia (October 1935) and Albania (April 1939), as well as giving aid to Franco's forces in the Spanish Civil War (1936 to 1939). To prepare for these campaigns Mussolini ordered a great rearmament programme starting in 1932; one result was the Autocarro Unificato, a standardised military truck made by all the important vehicle producers, Alfa Romeo, Bianchi, Fiat, Isotta-Fraschini, Lancia and OM. The idea was similar to the German Einheits Program, although the trucks did not exhibit the advanced design of their equivalents from north of the Alps. Nor was one design made by several different companies. Generally speaking the trucks were derived from civilian models. The specification laid down for the Autocarro Unificato series were as follows:-

Autocarro Unificato (Truck standardised)	Medio (Medium)	Pesante (Heavy)
Gross vehicle weight (kg)	6500	12,000
Payload, not less than (kg)	3000	6000
Engine type	Petrol or diesel	Diesel
Overall vehicle width, maximum (mm)	2340	2350
Body, internal dimensions (mm)	4000 x 2,000	4750 x 2,200
Ground clearance, minimum (mm)	200	200
Turning radius, minimum (mm)	7000	7000
Maximum road speed (km/h)	60	45★

★38km/h with 12-ton trailer.

Several more interesting, specifically military designs were the OM Autocaretta, the Breda artillery tractors and the various 4x4 tractors based on the ingenious design of Ing. Ugo Pavesi.

The war effectively ended for Italy in September 1943, with the fall of Mussolini followed by the surrender by Marshal Badoglio on 8 September. Thereafter, although fierce fighting still lay ahead for the Allies, Italy's Army, Navy and Air Force fought no more, and her industry was forced to produce war material solely for the Germans. This they did most reluctantly, for few Italians remained Fascists now and indeed serious strikes against the war had broken out at the Fiat works as early as March 1943. From September onwards the Fiat workers did everything they could to disrupt the production ordered by the Germans. They were supposed to deliver 180 aircraft a month, but never achieved more than 10% of this figure. Of the few trucks built, many disappeared mysteriously before they ever reached the Wehrmacht.

The German government became so impatient that in January 1944 they ordered that all Fiat machinery should be removed to Germany. This

only provoked a general strike over the whole of northern Italy and the order was never carried out. Later production became still more chaotic , and though Italian factories were in theory working for the Germans until April 1945, very little satisfactory material was turned out in the last six months.

Staff Cars

Some closed cars were used by the Italian armed forces, mainly for work within Italy, but the most typical staff car was the Torpedo Militare, an open four/five-seater tourer with a body somewhat similar to those of the German Kübelsitzer. During the 1930s Fiat had made several models of open tourer for cross-country use in colonial territories. These included two- and four-seater versions of the Tipo 508 Balilla and a five-seater on the Tipo 518 Ardita chassis. The two-seater Balilla was used by field commanders of small motorised units in the mid-1930s, but these colonial Fiats were not exclusively supplied for military purposes. In theory, they could be purchased by anyone wanting a rugged open touring car.

The next stage of Fiat Coloniale were more specifically military vehicles – the 508C Col and 508C Mil.1100. These were derived from the 508C Millecento introduced in 1937, which had a 32bhp, ohv engine and coil-spring independent front suspension. The 508C Col, made from 1937 to 1939, had a similar radiator grille, bonnet and

mudguards to the civilian model, with a four-seater four-door tourer body and twin spare tyres at the rear. Ground clearance was slightly higher than on the civilian version. The 508C Mil. made from 1939 to 1945 had a more utilitarian front end, step plates instead of running board and a lightweight tourer body which brought the overall laden weight down from 1,235kg to 1,152kg. The bonnet was generously louvred to provide adequate cooling in desert conditions.

The other military Fiat was the 2800 Mil. Col. based on the rare 2.8-litre six-cylinder car which they introduced as their prestige model in 1938 and which never sold very well. Although you could buy a new civilian model as late as 1944 if you had the right contacts and credentials, only 620 were made. How many of these were the military version is not known, but it could be as much as a third of the total. The six-cylinder, ohv engine developed 85bhp and both civilian and military versions had coil-spring, independent front suspension, with semi-elliptics at the rear. At 118in the military car's wheelbase was 8in shorter than its civilian counterpart, although it is believed that some short-wheelbase chassis were supplied to custom coachbuilders like Pininfarina who built sports coupé bodies on them. The standard military body was an open five-seater, with accommodation for 70kg load in the boot. They had 7.50x18 tyres carried two spares (one on each side of the bonnet) and were made from 1939 to 1941, being widely used by senior officers in the Western Desert.

Above: **One of many basically civilian designs which conformed to the Autocarro Unificato programme was the OM Taurus, produced under licence from the Swiss Saurer company. This photo, taken on 14 May 1945, shows a German soldier checking a German-operated Taurus during the round up of German troops in Italy on 14 May 1945. It was a most unusual situation; an American (right) and a German soldier patrolled together, the German stopping German vehicles and the American, Allied vehicles.**

Right: **Alfa Romeo made a number of staff cars, the 6C Turismo which was similar to their civilian models, and this 6C Coloniale Militare. It used the same 2.5-litre twin-ohc six-cylinder engine as the Turismo, but had greater ground clearance and military type five-seater body. Only 152 were made, mostly in 1941/42.**
(NMM)

Above: **The SPA CL39 was a popular light truck for the Italian Army. Although it has a five-speed gearbox, top speed was only 25mph. This is the CLF39 (Carro Legero Fanteria = Light Truck for Infantry); early versions had solid tyres, and there was also a Coloniale model with larger pneumatic tyres than this model.**
(Bart Vanderveen Collection)

If the Fiat 2800 was the most favoured staff car for prestige purposes, surely the favourite among sporting enthusiasts, or rather their drivers, as officers did not normally chauffeur themselves, was the Alfa Romeo 6C2500 Col. This was based on the 2500 which used a 2443cc six-cylinder twin-overhead camshaft engine, and was made from 1939 to 1953. In civilian form the engine developed 95 or 105bhp according to the degree of tuning, but the military model had a maximum output of 90bhp at 4500rpm. Nevertheless it had a top speed of 79mph compared with 71mph for the Fiat 2800. The body style was generally similar to the Fiat's, being a four-door five-seater tourer with twin spare wheels mounted at the sides of the bonnet. Passengers were expected to be more agile than those who rode in the Fiat, for neither running board nor step plates were provided and the ground clearance was $10^{1}/_{4}$in. The chassis was advanced for its day with all-round independent suspension, by coil springs

at the front and torsion bars at the rear. Unlike the civilian models the 2500 Coloniale had a radiator for cooling the oil, a tall, narrow structure mounted inside the water radiator core. The prototype was built in 1939, but most of the 152 cars made were delivered in 1941 and 1942. Thereafter Alfa Romeo were too busy making heavy trucks and other war material to continue production of this interesting staff car.

Two other companies which provided staff cars to the Italian Army were Bianchi and Lancia. The former made two models, the S9M which was based on their four-cylinder 1.5-litre S9 passenger car, and the S6M which was of similar appearance but used a 2.2-litre six-cylinder engine from a light commercial vehicle. Both had open tourer bodies, though the S6M was also made as a saloon. An S6M was used by Mussolini when touring the battle-fields in the early days of the war.

Lancia's contribution was a five-seater based on their well known Aprilia passenger car. It had a narrow-angle V4 engine of 1486cc developing 48bhp. As the ordinary Aprilia had unitary constuction the military tourers were built on the chassis which was made for taxicab and commercial bodies. They were similar in design to those used on other Italian chassis but carried only a single spare wheel which was mounted at the rear. The Aprilia was also made for the army with truck and ambulance bodies.

Light Trucks

There was no standardisation programme with Italian light trucks, and a variety of different models saw service. The lightest were members of that peculiarly Italian breed of vehicle, the motorcycle-based three-wheeler. These were first built in the

Left: **The extraordinary little OM Autocaretta which could be used as a light truck or artillery tractor. It was powered by a 1616cc air-cooled engine, and drove and steered on all four wheels. Most had solid tyres, as here, though pneumatics could be fitted. It was made from 1933 until about 1944.** *(Vehicle displayed at the Victory Memorial Museum)*

Centre: **The SPA CL39 was a light 4x2 truck for infantry support. Its engine was a surprisingly small four-cylinder unit of 1628cc. A variant was the CLF39 which had 700-18 solid tyres, while this example has 210-18 pneumatics.** *(Vehicle displayed at the Victory Memorial Museum)*

Left: **Fiat's 4x4 medium artillery tractor was made in the SPA factory and known as the TM40. Also available with solid tyres, it was powered by a 9365cc 110bhp six-cylinder engine. It was also made in truck form (T40) with German Einheits cab.** *(Vehicle displayed at the Victory Memorial Museum)*

Above: **A Breda Trattrice Pesante (Heavy Tractor) Tipo 32, powered by the company's own 8136cc four-cylinder petrol engine, and having a five-speed gearbox and four-wheel drive. It was built from 1932 to about 1939, when some were updated with pneumatic tyres and a diesel engine. Its successor was the Tipo 40.**
(Bart Vanderveen Collection)

was soon in production not only at OM's Brescia factory but also in Italy's east African province of Eritrea. Pneumatic tyres came eventually on the Tipo 36M of 1936 and there were also two personnel carrier versions, the 36P seating ten plus the driver and the 36DM seating seven plus the driver but also carrying an anti-aircraft gun. The Autocaretta remained in production until well into the war, and was highly thought of by Italian troops and also by British Army personnel who captured a number of them.

A similar 4x4 truck was made by another Fiat subsidiary, SPA (Societa Piemontese Automobili) of Turin. The SPA CL39 was slightly larger than

the Autocaretta and less radical in that it had a 1628cc water-cooled engine of and although it drove on all four wheels, only the front wheels steered. The original CL39 had 7.00x18 solid tyres (in 1939!), but the Coloniale model has 210x 18 pneumatics. Payload was 1ton. The centrally-mounted gearbox had five forward speeds, and top speed was 25mph. SPA also made a larger bonnetted 1-ton truck, the AS 37, powered by a 52bhp four-cylinder engine. This had all-round independent suspension by coil springs and four-wheel steering. It was made from 1937 to 1948 and included an artillery tractor version known as the TL37.

Medium and Heavy Trucks

In the mid-1930s the Italian War Ministry laid down specifications for medium and heavy military trucks to be built within certain standardised limits, as set out on page 188. Although the name Autocarro Unificato recalled the German Einheits Program, there was nothing like the degree of standardisation that prevailed in Germany, nor did several companies make the same design. But the biggest difference between the two schemes was that in Italy there were no modern designs produced to comply with the scheme, to compare with the 6x6 all-independent suspension vehicles provided for the Wehrmacht. The typical Autocarro Unificato was a basically civilian design

Right: **A Breda Tipo 51 heavy 6x4 chassis with Ansaldo 90/55 gun, abandoned near San Michele, Sicily, after the Allied invasion in July 1943.**
(IWM)

Left: **The extraordinary little OM Autocaretta which could be used as a light truck or artillery tractor. It was powered by a 1616cc air-cooled engine, and drove and steered on all four wheels. Most had solid tyres, as here, though pneumatics could be fitted. It was made from 1933 until about 1944.** *(Vehicle displayed at the Victory Memorial Museum)*

Centre: **The SPA CL39 was a light 4x2 truck for infantry support. Its engine was a surprisingly small four-cylinder unit of 1628cc. A variant was the CLF39 which had 700-18 solid tyres, while this example has 210-18 pneumatics.** *(Vehicle displayed at the Victory Memorial Museum)*

Left: **Fiat's 4x4 medium artillery tractor was made in the SPA factory and known as the TM40. Also available with solid tyres, it was powered by a 9365cc 110bhp six-cylinder engine. It was also made in truck form (T40) with German Einheits cab.** *(Vehicle displayed at the Victory Memorial Museum)*

1920s, and their descendants are still being made today, although in recent years the scooter rather than the motorcycle has been their basis. During the 1930s the best known makers of such machines were Gilera, Benelli and Moto Guzzi, and the latter two firms supplied three-wheelers to the Army. As far back as the saddle they were identical to an ordinary motorcycle, but drive was then from the single-cylinder engine and four-speed gearbox by shaft to a bevel-drive rear axle which carried an open or canvas tilt body with a payload of 1000kg. There were several body variants, including one to carry an anti-aircraft gun.

The standard light truck, similar in concept to the 'Tilly' of the British Army, was the Fiat 508C Mil. based on the passenger car, but with wooden half-doors and no side windows to the cab. The payload of the canvas tilt body was 350kg or about 7cwt, surprisingly low compared with the 19.8cwt payload of the Moto Guzzi three-wheeler. One version of the 508C Mil. was equipped with twin anti-aircraft machine guns. A larger Fiat truck was the 618 Mil. Col, a 25cwt vehicle closely based on the company's 618 civilian truck and made in two models, with coil or magneto ignition. It was in production from 1934 to 1937, but large numbers were still in army service during the war.

One of the most interesting Italian vehicles was the OM Autocaretta, built by Officine Meccaniche SpA of Brescia, a company which became a Fiat subsidiary in 1933. This highly individual vehicle was designed by Giulino Cesare Cappa who had been responsible for the 1906 Aquila Italiana, the first car to use aluminium pistons, Fiat's successful 803 and 804 racing cars of the early 1920s and the remarkable 1100cc V12 Itala racing car of 1926. The Autocaretta, whose prototype was built by Ansaldo, was a light forward-control 4x4 truck, powered by a 1616cc 21bhp four-cylinder air-cooled diesel engine. It was a curious mixture of old and new, having independent suspension all round, four-wheel steering, hand starting and solid tyres. The suspension was by transverse leaf springs above and below the differentials. Transmission was by a four-speed gearbox mounted centrally, which drove forward and backward to the two axles. A wheelbase of only 6ft 7in combined with four-wheel steering made the Autocaretta very manoeuvrable, and its cross-country performance was excellent. In the 1960s the light agricultural 4x4 became an Italian speciality, with a dozen or more firms offering such vehicles, but in 1932 it was remarkable and unique.

It may not have been conceived as a military vehicle but with the prevailing climate of rearmament it was inevitably taken up by the Army, and

Above: **In a similar class to the Alfa Romeo 800 was the Fiat 665/666 series, differing only in wheelbase, 665 with 376cm, and the 666 with 385cm. This is a 666NM, N indicating a diesel engine and M, military use. With a 9365cc diesel, they were rated for a 6 ton payload.**
(Fiat Centro Storico/ Nick Baldwin Collection)

Left: **An early version of the unusual OM Autocaretta, with solid tyres. Features included independent suspension with steering and drive on all four wheels.**
(Bart Vanderveen Collection)

the Autocaretta and less radical in that it had a 1628cc water-cooled engine of and although it drove on all four wheels, only the front wheels steered. The original CL39 had 7.00x18 solid tyres (in1939!), but the Coloniale model has 210x 18 pneumatics. Payload was 1ton. The centrally-mounted gearbox had five forward speeds, and top speed was 25mph. SPA also made a larger bonnetted 1-ton truck, the AS 37, powered by a 52bhp four-cylinder engine. This had all-round independent suspension by coil springs and four-wheel steering. It was made from 1937 to 1948 and included an artillery tractor version known as the TL37.

Medium and Heavy Trucks

In the mid-1930s the Italian War Ministry laid down specifications for medium and heavy military trucks to be built within certain standardised limits, as set out on page 188. Although the name Autocarro Unificato recalled the German Einheits Program, there was nothing like the degree of standardisation that prevailed in Germany, nor did several companies make the same design. But the biggest difference between the two schemes was that in Italy there were no modern designs produced to comply with the scheme, to compare with the 6x6 all-independent suspension vehicles provided for the Wehrmacht. The typical Autocarro Unificato was a basically civilian design

was soon in production not only at OM's Brescia factory but also in Italy's east African province of Eritrea. Pneumatic tyres came eventually on the Tipo 36M of 1936 and there were also two personnel carrier versions, the 36P seating ten plus the driver and the 36DM seating seven plus the driver but also carrying an anti-aircraft gun. The Autocaretta remained in production until well into the war, and was highly thought of by Italian troops and also by British Army personnel who captured a number of them.

A similar 4x4 truck was made by another Fiat subsidiary, SPA (Societa Piemontese Automobili) of Turin. The SPA CL39 was slightly larger than

which was accepted for the scheme so long as it conformed to the specification.

The medium category called for a payload of not less than 3 tons and a gross vehicle weight of $6^{1}/_{2}$ tons. Among manufacturers who supplied vehicles of this type were Alfa Romeo, Bianchi, Fiat, Isotta-Fraschini, Lancia and O.M. The Alfa Romeo was the 430 with six-cylinder petrol engine and a forward control cab. Similar in appearance was the 6-ton, 800RE with 108bhp six-cylinder diesel engine which fell into the AUP Autocarro Unificato Pesante or heavy category. The Bianchi Miles and Isotta-Fraschini D65 were semi-forward control trucks of basically civilian design as was the Fiat 626. This was available with a petrol (626B) or diesel (626N) engine and was widely used by the Italian Army and Air Force, and also the German Army. There was also a bus version designated the 626RNL. The OM Taurus was a bonnetted, 3-ton truck built under licence from the Swiss Saurer company and was available with a petrol (Taurus B) or diesel (Taurus N) engine.

Among suppliers to the AUP category were Alfa Romeo, Fiat, Isotta-Fraschini, Lancia and OM. Of these the Lancia 3Ro N Mil. was the most interesting for it was powered by a 6875cc five-cylinder ohv diesel engine built under patents from the German Junkers company. This unit, which was the first in-line five-cylinder engine until the 1960s (Unic) or 1970s (Audi and Mercedes-Benz), had Bosch direct fuel injection and developed 93bhp. It was the culmination of a line of Ro trucks which began in 1933 with the opposed-piston two-stroke two-cylinder 64bhp Ro NM. Some had solid tyres, and while their low speed prevented them from being accepted for the AUP class they were used by several Italian Army units alongside their younger sisters. The Ro NM had a four-speed gearbox with two-speed auxiliary box giving eight forward speeds, while the 3Ro N. Mil. had ten forward speeds. There was also a petrol version of this engine which could run on methane fuel. The 3 Ro N. Mil. was made from 1938 to 1946 and was the forerunner of a number of other five-cylinder Lancias made after the war. Most of these Unificato models had cargo carrying bodies, but they were also used as tankers, mobile workshops and recovery and communications vehicles.

Apart from the Unificato trucks, the Italian Army used a variety of other vehicles including older 4x2 trucks made by Fiat, Lancia and SPA, and more specialised 4x4, 6x4 and 6x6 trucks. Among the 4x2s was the $2^{1}/_{2}$-ton SPA 38R . This had a vintage appearance even when it was introduced in 1936, with vertical radiator and windscreen and half doors, and by the time it was phased out in 1948 it shared with the Russian ZIS-5 the distinction of being the most old-fashioned looking truck in the world. Nevertheless it was a widely used vehicle, made with a variety of bodywork including ambulance, workshop van, etc. It was powered by a 4053cc 55bhp four-cylinder Fiat engine.

Below: **Lancia 3 RO N powered by a 6875cc five-cylinder engine built under Junkers patents. It is carrying an Ansaldo 90/55 gun, and is fitted with ground supports to protect the chassis from the effects of recoil.**
(IWM)

Right: **The Fiat 626 had a smaller engine, of 5750cc, in petrol or diesel form, and came in two wheel-bases. This is a 628N built for the German Army in 1942, and has a German-made Einheits military cab.** *(Fiat Centro Storico/Nick Baldwin Collection)*

Army. Among the variants was a personnel carrier or mobile workshop with completely enclosed van bodywork by Viberti. The final development of the Dovunque series was the Tipo 41, a 6x6 powered by a 9.4-litre 115bhp six-cylinder diesel engine and rated for a 5 to 6 ton load. This was a handsome and versatile truck, with a top speed on metalled roads over 50mph and lockable central and axle differentials. Like all the Dovunque series, the Tipo 41 carried its spare wheels on stub axles between the front and leading rear axle, so that on rough terrain they acted as supports to prevent the frame from bottoming on humps. It was in production from 1943 to 1948.

Another truck on similar lines to the SPA Dovunque was the Breda, made by a large engineering combine, the Societa Ernesto Breda of Milan. Among road vehicles they were best known for their artillery tractors, but they also made 6x4 trucks from 1935 to 1945. The first were 3-ton trucks, but by 1940 they had grown to 7 tons with 8.8-litre six-cylinder diesel engines and air brakes. They were made as general load carriers and could also be equipped with a 90mm gun. In the latter case they were fitted with heavy stabilising outriggers to keep the vehicle steady when the gun was fired. Like the SPA Dovunque, the Breda 6x4 had spare wheels mounted at the side of the chassis capable of supporting it on rough ground.

Artillery Tractors

The first Italian heavy artillery tractors were developed during World War One, although Fiat had made singular examples as early as 1909. By the end of the war, Fiat were making a very powerful tractor capable of pulling two heavy artillery pieces (about 40 tons) cross-country or 100 tons on a good surface. Tractors were also made by La Moto-Aratrice to the design of Ugo Pavesi, an engineer who played an important part in the development of the road and agricultural tractor. The heart of Pavesi system was an articulated chassis that allowed the rear axle to swing independently of the front, both laterally and vertically. In effect there were two separate chassis of 200mm thick U-section girders, each carrying one axle. Steering was by a rack system on the front edge of the rear chassis. All wheels were driven, the front by chains from two shafts which ran from the gearbox, the rear by conventional propeller shaft from the gearbox to a differential above and behind the rear axle. Suspension was by eight coil springs at the rear and two at the front.

The first Pavesi had a flat-twin cylinder engine, but production models used a 9550cc four-cylinder engine and a two-ratio gearbox which gave speeds of 1.8 and 3.6mph. In the early 1920s this gave way to a three-speed box, with a top speed of 16mph.

The only 4x4 in the medium category was the Fiat/SPA T40, a 2½-ton truck derived from the TM40 artillery tractor. This truck had a 108bhp six-cylinder Fiat engine, five-speed gearbox and four-wheel steering. The tractor on which it was based had an open cab, but the T40 used an angular utility cab similar to that employed on some German trucks in the later years of the war.

The most interesting 6x4 trucks were the Dovunque series made by SPA but using many Fiat components. The name means 'Anywhere' and they were intended to combine good cross-country mobility and reasonable carrying capacity. The first Dovunques were made in 1933 and were quite small, with 2953cc 46bhp four-cylinder engines and a load capacity of 2 tons. Air brakes were used on early models, later replaced by hydraulics. By 1935 the Dovunque had a 4053cc 60bhp engine and was rated for a 2 to 3 ton load. The standard body was an open truck with canvas tilt and the forward control cab had a canvas top and no side windows. They looked not unlike the contemporary Guy and Karrier six-wheel trucks of the British

Drawbar pull was up to 100 tons on good surfaces and the Pavesi could be fitted with a 5-ton capacity winch, or a load carrying platform. The original tractor was only 8 feet long overall, but there were also load carrying tractor/trucks which were more than twice that length.

In 1924 the Italian Army ordered 45 Pavesi tractors, followed by a further order for 1,000 in 1925. The little factory in Milan could not cope with this, so production was taken up by Fiat who gave it to their specialist division, SPA. Manufacturing licences were taken out in Great Britain by Armstrong Siddeley, in Hungary by Manfred Weiss and also in Sweden. The Armstrong Siddeley version had pneumatic tyres, but most Pavesis used by the Italian Army had solids, sometimes dual solids at front and rear which spread the weight when the tractor was being driven on sand or mud. The final development was the P4-100, made from 1936 to 1942, and widely used by the Italian and German Armies. It had a smaller engine than its predecessors, a 4724cc four-cylinder engine developing 55bhp driving a gearbox with four forward speeds and an overall length of 13ft 6in. The P4-100 could tow loads up to 3$\frac{1}{2}$ tons on rough ground, 12 tons on well surfaced hilly roads and up to 75 tons on level ground.

In 1932 the Breda concern launched their Tipo 32, a 4x4 heavy road tractor powered by an 8136cc four-cylinder ohv engine which developed 84bhp. It had a five-speed gearbox from which separate driveshafts transmitted power to the wheels. The brakes were mounted centrally on the sides of the transmission below the cab. Each wheel had independent suspension, and was shod with 205x980 Celeglex semi-pneumatic tyres, twins on the rear wheels. Towing capacity varied from 5 to over 7 tons depending on the surface, and as a truck the Breda 32 could carry a 3$\frac{1}{2}$ ton load. A variant was the Tipo 33 which had a larger wheelbase and was used for carrying bridging equipment, some of which could be mounted on a four-wheel drawbar trailer.

In 1940 a new Breda tractor appeared, the Tipo 40 powered by a 110bhp five-cylinder diesel engine and fitted with 50x9 pneumatic tyres. As well as making new tractors of this type, Breda converted a number of their Tipo 32s to the Tipo 40 specifications. They were made with open or closed cabs and with or without a small cargo body behind the cab.

In addition to making the Pavesi-designed tractors, SPA built a number of machines of their own design, in two versions. The TL37 was a bonnetted tractor powered by a 4053cc, 57bhp four-cylinder engine with four-wheel steering and the option of pneumatic or semi-pneumatic tyres. It was also made with a light truck body for a 1 ton payload. The other SPA design was the TM40, a forward-control tractor with 108bhp six-cylinder diesel engine intended for towing loads of 5 tons, compared with 3 tons for the TL37. Like the latter, the TM40 had its truck equivalent which was fitted with a simple cab while the tractor was entirely open. It had accommodation for a crew of six, with an ammunition storage compartment behind. A similar design was prepared by Alfa Romeo, but it was SPA who were awarded the contact to build it in quantity.

In addition to their native designs, the Italians built a number of halftrack personnel carriers/tractors of German design. The Fiat 727SC was largely experimental, but Breda produced several hundred of their Tipo 61 which was a close copy of the Sd.Kfz. 7 as built by Büssing-NAG, Krauss-Maffei and Daimler Benz. It was powered by a 140bhp six-cylinder Breda-T14 engine.

Right: **Apart from the Breda Tipo 61 which was a close copy of the German medium halftracked tractors, the only Italian version of this design was the Fiat 727SC trattore semi-cingolato (half tracked tractor). It was powered by a Fiat 5750cc six-cylinder petrol engine and had a five-speed gearbox with reduction gear, giving ten forward-speeds in all. The prototype was built in 1942 and production began in 1943, but few were made before Italy's withdrawal from the war. It seems that the Wehrmacht did not take any Fiat halftracks, though they did use the Breda version which was much closer to their own designs.**
(Fiat Centro Storico/Nick Baldwin Collection)

CHAPTER EIGHT

Japan

Up to a month or so before the attack on Pearl Harbour Japan was still receiving large quantities of scrap iron from the United States.

onsidering its pre-eminent position today, it is surprising how young the Japanese motor industry is. In 1929 American companies in Japan assembled about 30,000 cars while the native manufacturers accounted for only 437. This did not please the intensely patriotic and militaristic Imperial Government, and it was particularly galling that they had to use mostly American equipment during their Manchurian campaign in 1931. The same year a Motor Industry Establishment Committee was set up to produce specifications for a standardised medium truck which would be suitable for civilian or military work. A new company was set up to manufacture these which integrated the military vehicle activities of DAT (later makers of the Datsun) and Ishikawajima. The company was called Kyodo Kokusan Jidosha KK, and their products were named after a sacred river, the Isuzu. A 4x2, the TX and a 6x4, the Type 94, were the first products and the latter became the most widely used Japanese army truck.

Foreign influence was scaled down in the 1930s in the same way as it was in Nazi Germany. In 1936 the Motor Car Manufacturing Enterprise Law stipulated that 50% of the capital, company officials and shareholders in any motor company should be Japanese and that they should follow any instructions that the army might give them. Three years later the Foreign Exchange Control law prevented the assembly of foreign vehicles, which meant American, altogether.

By this time the Japanese industry was well established, the leading companies being Nissan (formerly DAT), Isuzu and Toyota. In 1941/42 they built 45,433 trucks and buses, over 50% of which went to the armed forces. Passenger car production amounted to only 1,065. This was, in fact, the industry's best year until 1953 and the later war years saw a drop in production to 36,483 in 1942/43, 25,672 in 1943/44, 21,743 in 1944/45 and only 6,726 from April to August 1945. These figures are for commercial vehicles: car production never reached four figures during this period and no cars at all were made between April 1945 and early 1947. Vehicle production was hampered not only by bombing raids but also by demand for aero engines from firms like Nissan and Toyota and shortage of raw materials. (Up to a month or so before the attack on Pearl Harbour Japan was still receiving large quantities of scrap iron from the United States.) However, particularly in the first two years of the war, the Japanese were able to supplement their vehicle fleet with large numbers of American and British machines captured during their advances through the Philippines and Malaya.

Staff Cars

Many of the staff cars used by the Japanese forces were American machines which had been built under licence, or imported during the 1930s. Of the Japanese designs there were three categories (1)

civilian designs, (2) 4x4 and 6x4 command cars built for military use, and (3) small 4x4 scout cars.

Of the civilian designs, three in particular were favoured by the army, the Chiyoda H, Nissan 70 and Toyota AB. The Chiyoda was a large car of American appearance powered by a six-cylinder engine of about 4-litres, made in saloon and open tourer form. It was built by the vehicle division of the Tokyo Gas & Electric Company, and was named after the residence of the Imperial Household which had bought a TGE truck in 1931. Few were made, probably less than a hundred, and it seems to have had the same position on the Japanese market as the ZIS-101 had in Russia, in that it could not be bought openly, but was provided for important government and military personnel. The Nissan 70 was almost identical to the 1935 American Graham, as the Detroit company had sold the engine tooling and body dies to Nissan for $390,000. The 70 was made in saloon form from 1937 to 1940, while a seven-seater military tourer was built in small numbers in 1939. The Toyota AB and ABR were curious looking cars with a waterfall grille reminiscent of the 1935 Chrysler Airflow. Unfortunately the Toyota stylist lacked the courage to go the whole way towards streamlining and the headlamps were mounted separately from the bonnet sides in the old fashioned way, which gave an unhappy effect. Powered by a 3389cc six-cylinder ohv engine of Chevrolet design, the Toyota was made as a saloon (AA), tourer (AB) and military tourer (ABR). The latter

had cut away mudguards and other small modifications but was generally similar to the AB.

Two 4x4 command car designs were used, the Isuzu KIJ1 and the Mitsubishi Fuso BX33. Both used commercial vehicle components as the companies were not making passenger cars at the time, though both are now well known for their cars. The Mitsubishi was made by the motor division of the Mitsubishi Kobe Dockyard Works, another division of which made the famous Zero. It was a large open tourer with seven-seater bodywork. The Isuzu was generally similar, but unusual in being made with a diesel as well as a petrol engine. The latter was a 70bhp six-cylinder unit giving a top speed of 50mph, while the 55bhp four-cylinder diesel propelled the car at a maximum of 46mph. Both cars were made in the 1930s, at which time the Japanese authorities imported two German 4x4 designs for evaluation, the Mercedes-Benz G5 and the extraordinary Tempo G1200 with a pair of two-cylinder engines, one at each end of the car and driving separate axles.

The 6x4 command cars preceded the 4x4s and were inspired not by their German contemporaries as might be supposed, but by some six-wheeled cars which the Hudson Motor Car Co of Detroit had supplied for use in the Manchurian campaign. The Hudsons drove on one axle only, but otherwise they were generally similar to the Japanese designs made by Chiyoda, Isuzu and Sumida, all having large, open, seven-passenger bodies and six-cylinder engines.

Above: **The Isuzu Type 94 was a 6x4 with a capacity rating of 1½ tons. This seems low for general use, but normal for cross-country work for which the Isuzu was intended. There were some forty body variants, as well as a forward-control model, a 4x4 and a diesel option.**
(Bart Vanderveen Collection)

Above: **The Kurogane V-twin scout car with three-seater cloverleaf body. There was also a truck version, and experimental models featured four-door bodies and four-cylinder engines.**
(Bart Vanderveen Collection)

Right: **The Nissan 180 1½-ton truck was made in large numbers from 1941 to 1944, and revived after the war to be continued into the 1950s. It used a Graham-inspired 3670cc six-cylinder side-valve engine. Other bodies included tankers and fire trucks.**
(Bart Vanderveen Collection)

Three manufacturers submitted designs for the small 4x4 scout car class, Kurogane, Rikuo and Toyota, but only the first went into production. Kurogane was the trade name for the products of the Nippon Nainenki Seiko Company. Apart from the scout car, the company concentrated on three-wheeled commercial vehicles. Known as the Black Medal, or Type 95, the scout car was powered by a 1399cc air-cooled V-twin engine which developed 33bhp. The sump, crankcase, clutch housing and gearbox casing were all of aluminium and lubrication was on the dry-sump principle. The three-speed non-synchromesh gearbox was built in unit with the engine. Below the gearbox was the transfer box from which there was a centrally located driveshaft to the front axle and a normal propeller shaft to the semi-floating rear axle. Engagement of four-wheel drive was by a lever to the right of the gearbox.

The chassis consisted of a main backbone frame and two channel section side members only 10¾in apart, together with five cross members. Front suspension was independent by coil springs and wishbones, while at the rear there were conventional semi-elliptic leaf springs. Surprisingly, the brakes operated on the rear wheels only, with a handbrake working on the transmission. Top speed was given as 43mph.

The Kurogane Black Medal was made from

1939 to about 1943, the first models having two-seater bodies and later ones a cloverleaf three-seater. There were also a few with closed cabs and light truck bodies. They were widely used in the Burmese and Indo-Chinese campaigns and some captured examples were used by the French in their Indo-China war up to the mid-1950s. Total production was 4775.

Trucks

The smallest trucks used by the Japanese Army were three-wheelers using the front portion of a motorcycle, similar in concept to the Italian Moto-Guzzi . The motorcycle-based three-wheeler was a very important aspect of the Japanese industry from 1930 until the mid-1960s. They paid a low annual tax, were easy to drive and ideal for the narrow streets of Japanese cities. Up to 1937, and again from 1950 to 1955, more three-wheelers were made than four-wheelers, cars and commercial vehicles combined. The most common of these 'Sanrinshas' in military service was the Kurogane which used a similar V-twin engine to that employed in the Black Medal scout car, with three-speed gearbox and shaft drive to the rear axle. The standard body was an open sided truck with hinged tailgate, but water-carrying and other versions were also used. Smaller 'Sanrinshas' were made by Daihatsu and Mazda.

The four-wheeled pick-up class of vehicle was provided by the Kurogane Black Medal and the Toyota AK10, a 15cwt truck using many components from the AA passenger car. In the medium 4x2 truck category the main suppliers were Nissan and Toyota. Nissan made the attractive looking semi-forward control Type 80, a 1½-ton truck based on the American Federal and powered by the 3670cc six-cylinder engine used in the Type 70 car. As this was made from Graham tooling, the Nissan 80 was an American cocktail of a truck, but it was popular with both civilian and military users. Made from 1936 to 1938, it was superseded by the Type 180 which had the same engine under a normal full-length bonnet. The wheelbase and overall length were greater, yet the carrying capacity was the same. Presumably the advantage of the 180 lay in better engine accessibility, and this would have been a particularly important factor in military service. The 180 was made in considerable numbers from 1938 until the early 1950s.

Toyota supplied large numbers of trucks in the 1½ and 2 ton categories, mostly conventional models designed initially for the civilian market. The G series 1½ ton, appeared in 1935 as the G1 and was superseded by the GA and GB which were made up to 1942. Although they had Japanese designed bonnets and cabs, mechanically they were very similar to the contemporary Chevrolet, with 3.4-litre six-cylinder ohv engines and four-speed gearboxes. They were succeeded by the KB and KC which was generally similar but had a more powerful engine developing 78bhp. Altogether over 40,000 of these 1½-ton Toyotas were made between 1935 and 1944, and the KB was revived after the war. The KC had a 4x4 derivative, the KCY, and a number of amphibious load carriers were built on this chassis. 'On' was the operative word, for the bodies sat on top of the chassis, unlike the American DUKW, whose bodywork was built up around the chassis. The front and rear differentials were clearly visible below the hull. A total of 198 of these Toyota SUKI amphibians were made, between November 1943 and August 1944.

Isuzu trucks were on the whole heavier than Toyotas or Nissans, though the first standardised Japanese truck was the 1½-ton 6x4 Isuzu Type 94, which was made from 1934 to about 1941. Its type number was taken from the year of its introduction, 2594 of the Japanese calendar. The army became interested in the better cross-country performance of the 6x4 truck in the early 1930s, and from 1931 onwards they imported some of these vehicles, from Scammell and Thornycroft in England and from Tatra in Czechoslovakia. The Isuzu Type 94 was the result of their studies, although it was smaller than any of the imported trucks, with a capacity of only 1½ tons. It was made in 4x2 as well as 6x4 form, although the latter was more common. The engine was a 70bhp six-cylinder unit of 4.4-litres capacity, driving through a four-speed gearbox. Unlike many 6x4s, the Isuzu had single tyres all round. Most military versions had open cabs with canvas tops. As well as being used as a general load carrier, the Type 94s were fitted with special bodies such as searchlight carriers, workshops and aircraft refuelling tankers and were also used as artillery tractors.

There were several larger models of Isuzu, including the 2-ton YOK1 4x4 and ROK1 6x6; the 3-ton 2601 6x4; 7-ton Type 2 4x2 and the 20-ton dump truck, TH10. The Type 2 had an 8550cc six-cylinder diesel engine and five-speed gearbox. With a gross laden weight of nearly 13 tons, it was the heaviest Japanese truck in general use and was the basis for post-war Isuzu trucks.

Artillery Tractors

Like the Russians, the Japanese made great use of tracked vehicles for pulling artillery. Their first was the Sumida Type 92, a large and powerful full-tracked tractor not unlike the Russian Stalinets 65. The original version, the Type 92A, had a six-cylinder petrol engine, but it was succeeded by the diesel-powered 92B which remained in production until the early years of the war. This 105bhp six-cylinder power unit was made by Isuzu. A larger Sumida Type 92, for pulling up to 8 tons, used a 120bhp six-cylinder diesel engine made by the Nigata & Kubota Iron Works. This was the smallest in a range of standardised diesel engines, all with cylinder dimensions of 120x160 mm. Large tractors included the medium type with 160bhp 14,470cc V8 engine, and the heavy with 200bhp 21,703cc V12 engine. These tractors were less agricultural looking than the Sumida, with short bonnets and accommodation for a crew of seven. They were used for pulling 105 to 150mm Howitzers and 150mm field guns. The standardised 10,850cc six-cylinder diesel engine was also used in the Isuzu and KO-H1 Type 98 halftrack tractors. These had a crew of fifteen men and were used for pulling anti-aircraft guns. Introduced in 1938 they had a top speed of 28mph. The KO-H1 could be used as a gun carriage for an anti-aircraft gun, as well as for towing purposes.

Left: **Ikegai KO-HI 5-Ton halftrack tractor, intended as an AA gun tractor with a crew of fifteen. It was powered by a 110bhp six-cylinder diesel engine.**
(Bart Vanderveen Collection)

Index

Reference to photographs shown in *italics*

An experimental DUKW, the Scorpion, fitted with a 4.5mm rocket launcher which could fire 120 rounds in a few seconds.

Allied airborne troops aboard a Jeep and trailer leave their wrecked Airspeed Horsa glider. Ranville, Normandy 1944.

(Airborne Forces Museum, Aldershot)